<<<<<<<<>>>>>>>>

You're the Coach

Coach

The Transformational Power of Business Coaching

<<<<<<<<>>>>>>>>

W. Bradford Swift

Acknowledgments

My thanks go to the many people who in one way or another contributed to this book being written, starting with the person who introduced me to the idea of coaching, Judy Billman. She has made a profound difference in my life and in the lives of thousands of others through her compassionate skills as a coach.

I also thank my wife, Ann, for believing in me and for putting up with my idiosyncrasies in her caring, nonjudgmental way.

My heartfelt thanks also go to all my staff members who patiently experimented with me in what it takes to create a climate of coaching in a business setting, and that goes especially for Donna and Kathy.

The primary purpose of an organization is not to make a profit. It is to help human beings grow, express their creativity, contribute their life-force and make the world a better place. The purpose of an organization is to inspire the soul. ~ Leadership expert and Fortune 500 Business Consultant, Lance Secretan

Table of Contents

Foreword

One of the things that excites me as a veterinarian is the opportunity to network and exchange ideas with practitioners from around the world. It's a wonderful experience to help others and in turn have them willing to do the same. Such has been my relationship with Dr. Brad Swift. Over the years we've had the opportunity to open doors for each other — doors that have significantly contributed to our success.

Brad introduced me to the world of coaching in the late 1980s. He caught my attention when he shared stories of practitioners who were producing twice that of their colleagues in the same geographic area. Well, that was enough for me to request a meeting with Brad's coach, Judy Billman, who later became my first coach as well.

I can remember my first session with Judy, when we discussed what I wanted to accomplish. I decided to shoot for doubling the gross production in our two-doctor practice within a year, a goal that seemed impossible to me. To make a long story short, we didn't achieve that goal in one year, we did it in two — *as a one-doctor practice and with a staff that was one-third smaller.* You'd better believe there is incredible power and potential through coaching.

But I would be remiss if I stopped there. Brad opened a world that has transformed my life and that of my team, both personally and professionally. Since working with Judy we've continued to work with other coaches — in fact, it has become a way of life for us. The practice and our working relationships have improved greatly, thanks to our ability to communicate, lead, and work as teams. We've truly created an environment where people are honored, appreciated, and respected.

Over the past several years a lot has been said about Self-Directed Work Teams, Self-Managing Teams, Continuous Quality Improvement, and so on, yet a key ingredient often is left out: effective coaching. What Brad offers in this book is an opportunity for you to make a positive impact on your practice by taking these principles and running with them. Welcome to the world of coaching and teamwork.

Tim Banker, DVM
Fellow, Academy of Veterinary Dentistry
Greensboro, N. C.

Introduction: How it All Began

"Hello, my name is Judy Billman," the woman said as she held out her hand. *Pleasant person*, I thought, as I took her hand in mine. Judy had been referred to me by a pharmaceutical salesman who knew I was looking for a business consultant. His wife, another veterinarian, recommended Judy highly. One comment I remember well: "She's expensive and she's worth every cent." I didn't particularly like the "expensive" part, but I figured it wouldn't hurt to talk to Judy. If she was too expensive, I'd just plead poverty and send her on her way.

That was in 1988 and I'd been in my own professional practice almost eight years. Although the practice had done okay and by the community's standard I was a successful professional, I wasn't satisfied. As far as I was concerned, I worked far too many hours for far too little pay; plus my enthusiasm for my business had begun to wane. I finally began to consider that maybe, just maybe, I didn't know everything there was to know about running a business. After all, I hadn't taken one business course in college.

So with a big swallow of pride, I sent out the word that I planned to hire a business consultant. Although I considered several other consultants before talking to Judy, something about her intrigued me from the beginning — a crispness to her speech, a quiet confidence, and a pleasant sense of humor. Somehow Judy had been able to communicate all that in our initial phone conversation, and when I later spoke with her in person I was even more impressed…until we came to her fee. Then I was really impressed, and a little depressed as well. To paraphrase my colleague and Judy's client who'd referred her, "She expensive…and well worth it." I sure hoped that was true.

But strangely enough, even as I was trying to catch my breath, I knew I'd somehow find the money to hire Judy. I simply was too intrigued by what we'd covered in our hour-long meeting not to. So right then, I agreed to a six-month contract.

At the time I thought I'd hired a business consultant. You know the type — someone who would study my financial books and show me how to make the checkbook balance and pay myself more. Someone who would show me tricks on how to reduce my inventory so the drug companies wouldn't bleed so much of the financial life blood from the practice. The normal things you'd expect from a consultant.

Consultant versus Coach

Wrong. Judy isn't your typical business consultant. She's a business coach-the first one I'd ever met. Over the next three months, I had come to appreciate the difference between a coach and a consultant, but in the beginning I spent most of the time mystified by it all.

We hardly even glanced at the books those first three months, nor did we do much with the inventory. Instead, we spent a lot of time discussing me and the way I ran my clinic. Rather than tell me how to reduce my drug bills, Judy asked me such questions as, "What do you think the clients who no longer come to you say about you to their neighbors?"

Of course, I had no idea, so for several weeks I spent at least an hour a day calling inactive clients — people who for one reason or another had stopped coming to my practice. Oh, how I hated making those calls. As long as I didn't know why clients didn't return, I could pretend it was because they'd moved away, or because their pet had died, or because a relative had graduated from veterinary school and they'd been forced to switch veterinarians to keep the family peace.

While some of the people I called *did* give the first two reasons, many others did not. Although it wasn't easy for me to do, Judy "coached" me to develop these conversations so that everyone felt free to tell me the truth, not what they thought I wanted to hear.

One thing in my favor was that I was very coachable. After all, I was paying Judy an obscene amount of money to coach me. What was I going to do, ignore her guidance? Not hardly. So I gave my former clients plenty of room to say whatever they hadn't been able to say before — and believe me, they said it.

"Well, frankly, Dr. Swift, if you really want to know why I didn't come back…well, your place smells and it wasn't always as clean as I thought a hospital should be…."

"Dr. Swift, the last two times I came in to see you, you couldn't remember my name nor my pet's name, even though I'd been coming to see you for years…."

"To tell you the truth, I think you charge too much…."

I felt quite uncomfortable during these conversations, but Judy encouraged me to keep making the calls and let people speak their mind. She wanted me to listen carefully, take notes and, when appropriate, apologize. What she didn't want me to do was defend my past behavior or try to talk people into coming back.

We debriefed the phone calls each week when Judy traveled from her office in Charlotte, N.C., to meet with me for our three-hour coaching session. "What did you learn this week?" she'd ask, after settling in with a cup of hot tea. I'd sit there at my desk with the door closed, my face buried in a note pad, embarrassed and unsure where to begin. Finally, I'd just start talking and Judy...well, Judy listened, but in a way I'd never experienced anyone listen before. She didn't judge, she didn't laugh or make fun of me. She just listened with absolute attention and compassion.

More than once during these sessions, I broke down in tears. I didn't enjoy looking at my "darker side" — at my rudeness, arrogance, and lack of compassion with clients who'd finally grown sick of it and gone elsewhere. My tears only made things worse, heaping embarrassment on top of upset. And yet the coaching sessions continued, week in and week out.

Did I Make a Mistake?

Meanwhile, not much else was happening in the practice. Early on, Judy had instructed me to keep a running total of our average daily income so that we could track our results on a graph, but the line remained flat. Worse, the checkbook balance continued to plummet, in part because of the added expense of paying Judy.

After about two months, I grew worried. *Had I made a mistake? Had Judy paid my veterinary friend to say kind things about her? Maybe her style of consulting didn't work with me.*

But each week Judy returned with the same sense of purpose. She wasn't worried, so why should I be? (It wasn't until much later that Judy confided she too had been concerned about the lack of results and frequently consulted with her partner to figure out what was going on.)

Then the dam burst. Actually, it was more like a little leak, but it was a start. It was February, three months after I'd hired Judy. For the first time, my practice did better than it had the previous February. Not by much, but by that time, even a small gain gave us reason to rejoice. The next month was even better, and by April we were in full swing. By the end of the year, my practice had grown by more than 40 percent. And my personal income, even after paying Judy's fee, had more than doubled.

What was even more amazing was that we made these gains with a smaller staff and by working fewer hours. I used to come to the clinic around 8 a.m. and often not leave until well after six. But that year I began coming in at nine or so and left most nights right at six.

Most astonishing of all, I fell back in love with my business. I didn't expect to feel that way, especially after recalling my reaction to a question Judy asked me at our initial meeting: "Do you want to continue to practice?"

"No," I replied, "but I don't want to sell out either. I wouldn't feel that I was a success. It would be like sneaking out the back door." After thinking for a moment, I continued: "I'm ready to sell the practice and move on to something else, but not until I've built the practice to where it should be. I want to go out the top, not out the back door."

For the rest of the year we worked on that commitment so that I'd be able to sell the practice for a good price. But life is funny. At one point, when the practice was flourishing and I was having so much fun, I reconsidered Judy's question and learned what it's like to truly have a choice. It was as if someone had offered me a choice between a chocolate ice cream cone and a vanilla one. And being just as fond of chocolate as I am of vanilla, I couldn't go wrong. Now *that's* a position of freedom.

I eventually chose to sell my practice and thought long and hard about how to tell my staff, realizing that it would be one of the hardest things I'd ever do. My colleagues warned me that I'd be committing business suicide if I announced the news before I had a buyer, but I wanted to be upfront with my employees. Most of them had been with me through thick and thin, and we'd built the practice together.

So with careful planning and coaching from Judy, I told the staff of my decision the following spring. Despite the conventional wisdom that said it was impossible, we managed to maintain our phenomenal growth even while the practice was on the market. I credit this extraordinary result to the power of coaching.

The Transformational Power of Coaching

This book is about that power — the difference creating a climate of coaching can make in a professional, service-oriented business. While my examples focus on the business of running a veterinary clinic, this book is really for all professional business owners. Whether you're a dentist, accountant, chiropractor, attorney, medical doctor, veterinarian or other professional business owner, you will benefit from the material. I've seen the same coaching principles work for all kinds of businesses, from one-person operations to mega-corporations the size of AT&T. The only requirement: The business owner must be "coachable." This point is so important that the first chapter explores not only what it takes to be a great coach but what it means to be coachable.

Although it took months of hard work for my practice to explode with unprecedented results, I know that coaching works and that the concept is here to stay. Before long, the question won't be, "What is a business coach?" but instead, "Who is your business coach?" You'll gain a strategic advantage in your business if you start practicing the principles of coaching today.

Section

<<<<<<<<>>>>>>>>

ONE

<<<<<<<<>>>>>>>>

Practice Peak Performance

CHAPTER 1

<<<<<<<<<>>>>>>>>

You're the Coach!

And that means your team is looking to you for guidance. Here's how to inspire peak performance.

For the last several decades every four years thousands of the world's finest athletes gather for the Summer Olympics. Although they come from many different countries, they all have one thing in common. They each bring along one or more coaches because all the athletes know that if you want to excel in sports and especially if you want to *go for the gold,* you need a good coach.

The same is true for business. Whether you're a seasoned practice owner, a recent graduate or small business owner this book is designed to coach you on how to become a master coach in your business. To get the most out of your reading, picture yourself in a locker room during half time, getting coached on how to excel in the second half. Then apply the coaching skills to your own situation.

To ease the transition from locker room to the field of play, I've included exercises at the end of each chapter. Although you may feel the urge to skip over them, as your coach I strongly recommend that you resist the temptation. The power of this book is in the exercises because it is through them that you'll begin to apply what you've learned. And that's the first step to enjoying a winning season with your team.

Why coaching works

A coach is someone whose ability to communicate helps his or her players accomplish results beyond those considered predictable. Although the coach doesn't actually engage in the performance, he or she has a significant impact on it.

As most of us have seen in sports, the right kind of coaching can alter a player and team's performance. Consider, for example, Boston Celtics coach Red Auerbach. In the 1950's, when Auerbach began coaching the Celtics, they were just another basketball team. Auerbach instilled "Celtic Pride," and they became champions. He changed the way the Celtics saw themselves, and how others saw them as well. Since that time, countless other coaches have conducted a similar transformation both for teams and individuals. The same is possible in business.

By creating a coaching climate in my practice, I found that my staff's performance exceeded my expectations—and the people didn't have to change for me to get these results. In fact, we were able to accomplish more with a leaner team. Without a coaching environment, most employees are only as good as their demonstrated talents. But when coached, they often exceed these levels. Why? Because they know what you expect from them and how to meet those expectations.

To become a coach to your employees and staff, let's observe what great coaches do, then put their winning strategies to work building a team that excels.

Uncovering your employee's commitment

A great coach is able to identify a "coachable" player — a

team member who displays a commitment to the game. How can you tell if you employ such players? As Woody Allen put it: "Eighty percent of life is showing up." If your staff shows up for work, you know they have at least some level of commitment. In the professional practices and most other small businesses that focus on service, it's unlikely that they come to work for the sole purpose of becoming rich. Many employees, in fact, may not even know why they are there. It's up to you as a coach to learn what makes them tick.

One way to discover an employee's commitment is to listen to what he or she says, even when complaining. If a staff member complains, yet makes suggestions or promises at the same time, you're hearing a commitment—and the sound of a coachable person. Listening for a staff member's commitment in a complaint is one of the most important steps in shifting to an environment where coaching can flourish.

A complaining staff member may not be aware of his or her commitment. When I first shifted the way I listened to complaints from, "Oh, no, here we go again," to "This person is complaining out of a commitment to make this practice work," I realized that complaints present an opportunity to uncover problems that might otherwise interfere with my team's performance. Complaints also became an opportunity for me to coach my employees to excel.

For example, let's study this complaint: Your receptionist, Cindy, says in an exasperated voice, "That's the third no-show this afternoon. Why do clients bother making appointments if they're not going to keep them?"

On the surface, Cindy's complaint might irritate you. But when you think about it, only a person committed to your practice's success would be upset by clients failing to show up. Here's an opportunity to turn a complaint into committed action.

You might say, "Cindy, I can see you're really upset when clients don't keep their appointments, and I appreciate that you're so interested in seeing the practice do well. I'd like to talk with you about what we might do to cut down on all these broken appointments."

Your concern shows that you're talking to a committed team player. Remember: What you expect from people is usually what you get. Now that you know Cindy is a committed player, the two of you can talk about taking action to eliminate the cause of the complaint—the no-shows. This strategy is much more effective than if you'd decided what should be done and then delegated your ideas to the front-office staff.

Is your team listening to you?

Your best intentions as a coach can be tripped up by *how* your employees listen to you. It's human nature for an employee to hear coaching as criticism and then become defensive. A good coach overcomes this problem by taking the player's natural reactions into account—and getting the player to listen anyway.

For example, if you must discuss something that will likely upset an employee, and you know that if you were in that person's shoes you'd probably hear it as criticism, try starting the conversation this way: "What I'm about to tell you may be difficult to hear. I'm not saying it to be critical and it important that I be able to speak honestly to you so that I can point out something I've observed which is interfering with you being as effective as I know your committed to being." By bringing up the employee's commitment, you reduce the likelihood that he will take offense—and prepare him to listen openly to your coaching. We'll discuss listening skills in more detail in Chapter 12.

Coaches must listen, too

The best way to get your team to listen to you is to listen to them. Your employees will get the most out of your coaching if you "try on" what's being said and see the situation from the other person's perspective. You don't have to agree or disagree with the other person's perspective. Just consider it.

Suppose you want to establish a coaching relationship with a potential employee. After conducting second interviews, you're leaning toward hiring Avery Jones as a technician. Here's a sample conversation of how you might approach the subject of coaching: "Avery, I must say I'm impressed with your credentials and work experience, and your references are strong as well. I'm sure we also can work out a pay scale that's equitable. Before we proceed, I'd like to ask you one very important question. If you're hired for this position, what are you interested in providing for the business and for the rest of the staff?"

Listen carefully to Avery's response. He will tell you what he's committed to providing as an employee—and that will give you a good indication of how coachable Avery is.

"Well, Dr. McNeal, I want to be as good a technician as I'm capable of being. I'd like to continue to develop my skills so you'll feel comfortable giving me more responsibility, and with the increased responsibility I'd like to feel I'd be fairly compensated."

"And how about with the rest of the staff, Avery?"

"Well, I certainly want to get along with them and to fit in as part of the team. I'd also like for us to work without a lot of tension or gossiping."

"That's great, Avery. And I'd like for you to know that, as your employer, you can count on me to support you in all that you've just said. In fact, this is how I suggest we work together. Even though I'm your boss, with all that entails, I would prefer you consider me your coach. Someone who will assist you in accomplishing what you just said you want to achieve. Is that agreeable with you?"

"Well, it sure would be different from how I've related to other employers. Yes, I'm willing to give it a try."

"Great. Now, particularly in the early stages I may have a lot of suggestions for how I want you to perform your duties. It would be easy to hear them as though I'm being critical, but I'm going to ask that, in those moments, you to remember this conversation and realize that I'm coaching you to be as effective an employee as possible. Then consider what I'm saying with an open mind. Will you do that?"

Such conversations lay the groundwork for powerful relationships built upon mutually agreed upon commitments. The relationship you and I are establishing is no different. As your coach, I'm committed to whatever it is you want to achieve in your practice. I want to help you succeed, so listen to what I'm saying with an open mind. If you commit to learning all you can from the book, I believe you'll come away empowered—and ready to coach your team to a winning season.

EXERCISE

Think about these questions:

1. How do your employees relate to you? Look beyond such simple answers as "like I'm the boss." What kind of boss are you in their eyes? Then ask several staff members for their opinion of you as an employer. This exercise shows you how to make it safe for your staff to communicate with you.

Start by explaining to your employees that you want feedback about who you are as their employer and you want them to feel free to say what they truly think not just what they may perceive is the "right" answer. Ask them what works and what doesn't work. Promise to use whatever they say as useful feedback to improve yourself and that you will not use anything they say against them. Make sure you do not take the feedback personally but as a tool to make a difference. If it helps finds someone who is a confidant for you and use them to work through any disconcerting information you may receive.

2. How do you listen to other people? How do your employees, clients, and family members listen to you? At this point, simply record your observations.

A helpful suggestion here is to keep a notebook of your observations and feedback about what you are learning. Don't depend on just your memory to keep track of all this information. Memory can be fickled leaving us with inaccurate information.

3. What is your vision for your practice? How might you powerfully impact your daily activities and those of your employees? (Please note: Many of the exercises include such

questions, but try to avoid the natural tendency to come up with an answer as fast as possible and then quit. That's not the nature of these questions. Instead, make a mental note of whatever you come up with, or write it down, then move on and return to the questions later.) Keep this in your notebook.

Notes:

CHAPTER 2

<<<<<<<<<>>>>>>>>

Create a Vision

Defining your business mission clarifies your commitment to your team, your clients, and the community.

Like any successful coach, you need a powerful vision to guide your team, a clear declaration of your purpose and priorities. You don't have time to create a vision, you say? All your energy goes to putting out fires? Believe me, I know what that's like. I used to do the same thing. But after many years, I began to understand that if I didn't somehow find the time to change my ways—and get my priorities straight —I'd still be dousing those flames today. And I'd be even more burned out than I was back then.

Developing a vision turned my practice around. I pondered questions I'd never considered before—questions that made me take a close look at what I wanted from practice. What I thought would be a tedious chore actually ended up being an exhilarating experience.

That's why I urge you to find two hours a week when you're watching television or reading the newspaper to work on your vision instead. If you've already drafted a vision statement, review it now. Does it accurately reflect what you're committed to in your practice? Do your employees know the vision and agree with it? Does it inspire you and your staff? Feel free to adjust your vision as necessary, or even design a new one.

Brick by brick

Below you'll find a list of questions that will help you create your vision. To get the most out of the exercise, I recommend that you follow these six steps:

1. Ponder each question. You may find it useful to take a walk and "discuss" the questions with yourself. This stage may take you several days, so carry the questions with you on a note card.

2. Write down your responses in a notebook. It's natural for this stage to reveal insights you didn't have while pondering the questions. Schedule at least two 30-minute blocks to sit quietly and just write.

3. Discuss the questions with people you trust. Make a point to talk with all of your employees. They'll help you fulfill your vision, so the sooner you bring them into the conversation, the better. At this stage, all input is valid—you're simply exploring possibilities. Whatever you do, don't develop a vision without your team's input. If they don't accept the vision, then it will be impossible to accomplish.

4. Write down how others responded, along with anything new that occurs to you. Don't rush this process, but don't put it off either. Work on your vision a little bit every day.

5. Keep in mind that there are no "right" or "wrong" answers. Record your initial response to every question, then reread the questions. Be on the lookout for nuggets of inspiration—words, phrases, and ideas that grab your attention.

6. Don't worry if this process elicits ideas that are just the opposite of what you want. Exploring the possibilities sometimes sparks negativity. Just make note of such

thoughts and go on.

Be a visionary

Here are the questions to fuel your introspection:

• What do you love about your practice? Why did you choose the veterinary profession? Look beyond the financial aspects of your business. What else appealed to you? If you could redesign your practice, what would you add? What would you take away?

• What contributions would you like to make to others through your practice? Your list may involve your staff members, your clients, your community, or even the rest of the world. It also may include others in a similar business.

• Who do you want to be known as in your profession? What do you want to be known for? Your responses may focus on certain values, ways of operating as a business owner, or such descriptions as "most successful" or "most easy-going."

• If you had unlimited time, money, talent, and energy, what would you do with your practice? What would your business stand for? (Although selling your hospital is always an option, look beyond that answer for this exercise.)

• Imagine you're at the end of your professional career, and your staff and community are hosting a special dinner in your honor. What will they say about your accomplishments?

Call a vision meeting

By now, you should have several pages of notes. The next step is to meet with the people who will help develop the vision. Who you choose to work with at this stage is up to you. While it's a good idea to include as many employees as possible, too many participants will hamper the creative process.

If you have fewer than a dozen employees, consider meeting with everyone. If you have a larger staff, you could pick one or two staff members from each department or position. If you don't involve all of your employees, however, think about how you'll include them later. Whatever you do, don't a vision without your team's input. If they don't buy into the vision, the work will be impossible to accomplish.

To prepare for the meeting, go through your notes with a highlighter and mark words, phrases, and ideas that keep coming up as well as any common themes. If you get stuck, ask someone else to review your notes with you. Then write each word, phrase, or idea on a separate sheet of paper large enough so that everyone at the meeting can read them from several feet away.

Before you schedule the meeting, tell the participants you want to gather for, say, an hour to create a vision for the practice. Although you may be able to draft a powerful statement in one sitting, it will probably take two or three. The vision you create will become the driving force of your business, so don't rush through the process. At the same time, don't drag it out or you'll never finish it.

After the participants spend a few minutes reading the ideas from your notes, ask them to group the sheets of paper in similar categories, adding their own thoughts and phrases to the list. Then tape the sheets in a row on the wall and step back. Do you see any closely related words and phrases? Can you reduce the number of "columns" on the wall by placing similar terms underneath each other? For example, one sheet of paper may denote leadership in your field while another expresses your desire to be No. 1 in business. Can you move one sheet of paper under the other?

Your job is to facilitate this discussion and make sure everyone gets to contribute. Keep the atmosphere light and fun—if tempers flare, stop the meeting for a moment and reiterate that the purpose is to create a vision that everyone can accept. The idea is to end up with three to five columns of similar ideas on the wall.

Now ask the participants to eliminate as many redundant words and phrases in each column as possible. If an employee won't give up an idea even though the rest of the staff wants to toss it out, point out that everyone must sacrifice a little for the good of the group. The secret is to go with consensus.

If a staff member tries to delete an item from the list and the others object, that's a good sign you're close to being done with this stage. After that happens several times, thank everyone for participating and schedule a follow-up meeting in a few days. Or, if your team is up to it, you could take a short break and then go on to the next phase of the process.

Crystallizing the vision

Now it's time to connect all the remaining phrases. If more than eight people are present, divide them into groups of four to six and ask them to write a vision statement, using all the words on the wall. For a smaller group, each person can create a vision statement or work in teams of two.

Set a time limit of 20 to 30 minutes for this step, then ask each group or individual to read the vision statements aloud. Tell the participants to listen for sentences and phrases that inspire them, reminding them not to get too attached to their own version.

After all the statements have been read, ask the group to nominate the phrases, sentences, or entire vision statement they found most inspirational and that captures a vision they can endorse. Have someone write the selections on the wall, word for word. Then go over each one and ask for a show of hands if employees think it should remain there. Go with the majority. If one nomination seems similar to another already on the board, bring it to the group's attention and decide whether just one will suffice.

Once you have three to five statements on the wall, form a small "word-smithing" committee to combine the statements into a single, inspiring vision statement. Then ask an enthusiastic staff member to present the final version to the group.

This experience can be quite moving. For many people, it will be the first time they created something so powerful in a group setting. Best of all, taking part in such an activity brings your staff together—and turns them into a team with vision.

EXERCISE

Create an inspiring vision statement for your practice. You'll get more out of future chapters if you clarify your purpose before moving on. (For a sample vision statement, see Chapter 3.)

CHAPTER 3

<<<<<<<<<>>>>>>>>>

Turning Your Vision Into Reality

With your new vision statement in hand, you're ready to put words into action and fulfill your purpose through projects.

If you followed the coaching in the last chapter, you're part of a business with a vision. Congratulations! While I don't want to put a damper on your enthusiasm, I must warn you about a common pitfall at this point: The vision gets framed, mounted on the wall for all to see—and then forgotten.

I observed this phenomenon once when I walked into a large corporation. A beautiful poster in the reception area displayed an inspiring vision statement. As I read it, I was impressed by the company's commitment to customer service. But when I reached the reception desk, I was in for a rude awakening. The receptionist was on the phone, chatting with a friend. Although she noticed my arrival, she ignored me for several minutes until she'd completed her call. As a result, I was late for my appointment.

That company's vision statement obviously was nothing more than an attractive wall hanging. In this chapter, we will look at how to bring your business' vision into reality—and keep it alive.

From theory to practice

To make your vision an integral part of your business, you need to implement projects that reflect your intentions. Each project must offer specific, measurable results that clearly indicate whether you're fulfilling your objective. Let's look at a sample vision statement and develop appropriate projects for it:

Total Pet Care Clinic is dedicated to providing the highest level of service to patients and clients by:
- *Communicating openly and emphasizing preventive medicine;*
- *Showing that we care about all aspects of our patients' health and happiness;*
- *Being an active part of the community and an advocate for people's right to have and enjoy pets.*

In my opinion, the areas with the most potential for projects include: "highest level of service," "emphasizing being proactive on the customer's behalf,""going beyond the usual service,""active community involvement," and"advocate for people's right to have and enjoy pets."

For example, to show that you're "an advocate for people's right to have and enjoy pets," you could start an animal-assistance program for community health-care centers and retirement homes. The idea would be to provide these organizations with information on the health benefits of pet ownership. To measure the results, you could track the number of times you, your staff, or clients take animals to the facilities and how many residents you visit. Your goal might be to make at least 12 visits per year and see 250 people. Of course, this is just one example. The point is that when you create a powerful vision statement for your business, you can then create ways to express that vision through various projects.

Unlike simply posting pleasant words on your wall, designing projects that offer tangible results makes your vision a reality. "But how do such projects make my business money?" you may ask. It's true, not every project will directly add to the bottom line. But what such "socially responsible businesses" as Ben and Jerry's Ice Cream have realized is that being socially responsible is in itself good for business. The nursing-home project described above obviously doesn't have any clear profit motive built in. But don't you think your clients and others in the community would develop a positive image of your business if you and your employees worked on such a project? Don't you think your employees, who helped create your practice's vision statement, might get excited about doing something good for other people? Don't you think such effects might trickle down to the bottom line? You'd better believe it.

Of course, some projects will both fulfill your vision and directly enhance revenue. For instance, what products or services are you not offering that would contribute to "all aspects of our patients' health and happiness"? One answer may be dog obedience classes. A well-trained dog makes a better pet and is happier because it spends more time with its owner—and less time cooped up in the backyard.

If you don't already have an employee who's trained in dog obedience, your first goal would be to hire someone with that training or work out an arrangement with a local trainer. Another goal may be to hold the first class within 60 days and with at least 12 students. To measure the results, determine the additional revenue the classes bring in—and don't forget to keep track of how many new clients the classes attract.

Making promises—and keeping them

Projects are like the support beams used to shore up the opening to a mine. Without reinforcement, the hole would get filled in by the daily routine. Before you know it, your vision could be no more than a fond memory.

To stay true to your intentions, be public about your projects. Include your entire staff in the activities and invite your clients to participate. If you promise others you'll follow through, you're more likely to be successful.

I also suggest you seek the help of a "committed listener," someone who will listen to your promises each week and hold you to your word. He or she may be your coach/consultant, a colleague, an employee, or a family member. Just make sure this person isn't afraid to confront you if you start to slip. This type of relationship will help you build your "integrity muscle"—doing what you say, when you say it.

Does that mean you'll keep every promise? Probably not. In fact, if you're fulfilling all of your commitments, they may not challenging enough. A promise forces you to stretch a bit to fulfill it or it's only a prediction of what would have happened anyway. I don't need to promise that the sun will come up in the morning because I already know it will. However, I may need to promise my wife that I'll be up in time to see the sunrise with her.

If you don't follow through on a project, you must tell the people involved and find out what you can do to repair the situation. Let's say you're working on the dog obedience training project, and you promised your staff and your committed listener that you'd hire an experienced trainer by the end of June. But by July 1st you still haven't hired anyone. That creates a problem because your staff already lined up seven people to start classes the very next week. What do you do?

The first step is to level with your staff. If you're still committed to the idea of holding dog obedience classes, discuss a new time frame for hiring a trainer. The next step is to tell the seven people who signed up for the training that you've rescheduled the classes and apologize for the inconvenience. Note: Even if you delegate these calls to an employee, it's your responsibility to see that the job gets done. Finally, make hiring a trainer by the new deadline a top priority.

Be a show-off!

An excellent way to keep your vision thriving is to display your projects in an area where the entire staff can see them. Just imagine how tough it would be to play a whole season without knowing the score until the end of the game. How many professional players do you think would hang around to find out if their team was going to the finals?

Unfortunately, far too many business owners don't know where they stand—or realize how costly such a mistake can be. In the next chapter, we'll talk about how to design scoreboards that will keep your team in the know.

EXERCISE

Take two or three ideas from your vision statement and design three projects keeping these pointers in mind:

1. Make sure each project reflects a portion of your vision statement.

2. Specify measurable results for each project, including deadlines.

3. Choose the one you and your employees think would be the most fun and productive to complete.

4. Implement the project and track the results. Is the outcome what you expected? Are you on schedule? For the best results, don't take on the next project until the first one is fully operational.)

I also recommend that you find a committed listener to help you during this process. While you don't have to rely on the same person for every project, be sure to choose someone who will hold you to your commitments.

Notes:

CHAPTER 4

<<<<<<<<<<>>>>>>>>

Are You Winning?
Check the Scoreboard

Do you keep track of the score during the game—or only read about how your team did the next day?

The referee blows the whistle for timeout. As you run off the court with your team, your assistant coach tells you there are two minutes left in the game. As the coach, it's your responsibility to direct these last two minutes, to decide the strategy that will win the game. You glance at your team members' hot and sweaty faces, lit up with excitement. It's been a good game. They've given their best effort and a win would feel great.

Before you plan your strategy, you gaze up at the scoreboard—but the lights on the board are out. What's the score? Who's winning and by how much? You glance back at your teammates. They wait with smiles for your direction. But if you don't know the score, how do you coach them?

Sound ridiculous? How could anyone plan a game strategy without knowing the score? Well, thousands of business people do it day in and day out, often without realizing it.

I remember the first time my business consultant and I sat down to review my hospital's financial records. I proudly pulled out a thick notebook from my bookcase and blew away a thin layer of dust from its cover.

"When do you get this financial information from your accountant?" Judy Billman asked as she leafed through the pages.

"Usually within 30 to 45 days after the month ends," I replied with satisfaction. It had taken my former accountant 60 to 90 days.

"Well, getting the figures that long after the month ends is like reading a month-old newspaper to see how your team did in the big game," Judy said as she closed the notebook and set it on my desk. "It may make for interesting reading, but it has no impact on how you play the game."

The game of business

As I considered what Judy said, I realized that comparing business to a game made sense. I began to think of my staff as a team and my hospital as a playing field. My job as the coach was to help the team become a winning dynasty. Each month represented a separate game, giving us a playing season of one year, or 12 games.

I soon discovered that my financial notebook was nothing more than a report on how my team played during the past season—in fact, it could be more appropriately called our scrapbook. I also realized that even a computer printout run the first day of the following month provides little more than a recap of Sunday's game in the Monday morning newspaper.

What my team needed was a simple scoreboard we could check periodically as we played the game of running a veterinary practice. As a coach, it would be my responsibility to check the score from time to time throughout the month, and adjust our practice strategy accordingly.

I quickly learned that keeping an eye on the scoreboard

during the game can make a tremendous difference. In fact, when I began paying attention to the score, my practice grew more than 40 percent in one year; in previous years, we'd never grown more than 10 to 15 percent. Another bonus: My take-home pay doubled.

What a Scoreboard tells you

It's up to you to decide which numbers to display on your scoreboard. Most veterinarians agree that keeping track of daily production and collection figures is important, but another number gives you a better sense of your performance: net profit.

To determine your monthly net profit, first calculate your monthly expenses. How much money must you bring in each month to pay all the bills and keep your doors open? This number will vary from month to month, so it's a good idea to figure a quarterly average. You can refer to last year's numbers in your "scrapbook" and make adjustments for any significant changes this year, such as the addition of staff members.

I also recommend that you include your own salary in your calculations. Depending on the accounting method used, the owner's salary may come from the net profit as a draw. But in this game the coach should be paid just like a team member.

When you've determined your monthly expenses, you know how much money you have to make each month. If you make less than that figure in a given month, you lose that game; if you meet it, the game is a tie; and if you make more, you win the game.

Keep in mind that you don't have to show a net profit every month to have a winning season. On the other hand, if you have a long losing streak, you may find yourself out of the game, out of work, and out of business.

Vital team statistics

The most successful coaches watch more than just the scoreboard—they also pay attention to the team statistics: the percentage of baskets made, the number of rebounds, and so on. Developing your own set of team statistics will give you the means to fine-tune your team's performance.

Here are some of the statistics I monitored regularly and posted for my team to see:

• **Average daily production per week.** This figure smoothes out those weeks when your business is closed for holidays, providing a more accurate reflection of your production. To calculate, divide your gross production for the week by the number of days your practice was open, including any half-days during the weekend.

• **Number of clients seen per month and average client transaction.** For your practice to grow, you must see more clients and increase the service each client receives per visit. (Another option is to raise your fees, but that route doesn't reflect performance.) My practice grew 40 percent after we started seeing more pet owners and convinced clients to accept more services.

• **Number of new clients.** Thriving practices see a significant number of new clients. You won't know how many new clients you have, however, unless you track them. I also recommend tracking *how* new clients find you. Did they first see your ad in the Yellow Pages? Did they see your sign? Did their children hear you speak at school? Did a client refer them?

Make your statistics work for you

The above calculations are a good starting point, but after a while you may want to track specific areas, then switch to other statistics. For example, one of our team goals was to increase the number of new clients we saw. In the first few months of tracking, we found our numbers surprisingly low —something we wouldn't have known otherwise.

When we looked at how to generate more clients, we decided our best bet was to communicate more with potential clients and to distribute more business cards and hospital brochures. We knew we couldn't track everything, so we decided to track the number of business cards handed out and the number of times a staff member asked a client to send us a friend. The results were amazing: Within just a few weeks, our new-client numbers jumped from one to three a week, to five to seven.

Involve your team

By now, you may be wondering who has time to keep track of all these numbers. I know that's the first thing I asked Judy when she suggested it. At the time, I had no idea the difference keeping score was going to make in our earnings or in my take-home pay.

I quickly discovered, however, that keeping score is much easier when it's a team effort. Instead of tracking the numbers myself, I evaluated what the numbers meant and determined what actions to take. The tracking job went to my strongest team player, Donna, my receptionist. She'd been with me the longest and was the most committed to our success. She also had easy access to the numbers.

Donna compiled all of the basic data and gave me a

report at the end of the week. (I must admit that I occasionally looked over her shoulder to see how we were doing.) This system showed us where we were at the end of each week and gave us plenty of time to adjust our game plan *during* the game.

I put other employees in charge of special team statistics, such as the number of business cards we distributed. Each person managed one or two statistics. As long as they recorded the information accurately and regularly, they could decide how to track the numbers most effectively.

At the end of the week, I brought the team together to review our game, especially if we were behind. These meetings proved to be a great opportunity to coach the staff, acknowledge them for their hard work, and ask them to clear up any grievances. We also discussed specific cases that had either gone well or poorly from a client-relations perspective.

Looking back, I see that the decision to include everyone in the endeavor—something I'd never done before—made us a stronger team. Just imagine how frustrated *you* would be as a team member if only your coach knew the score during the game.

Design your scoreboards

A business scoreboard can be designed to tell you as much or as little as you want to know. I suggest you begin with something simple and refine them as you go along. Here are some of your options:

• **Grids** capture a lot of information on one sheet of paper, which gives you a good overview of how you're doing and draws attention to pieces of your game plan that may need attention before the end of the month.

The example below is only a starting point, but I suggest you begin with a line for the date and one for the number of working days. Not all "games" are the same length, so figuring the actual number of working days makes it easier to calculate the average production and collection figures for the month. In the example grid, the practice isn't open on weekends, and holidays are indicated with an "H."

To obtain the average daily production and the average daily collection figures at the end of the month, divide the monthly production total and the monthly collection total by the number of days your hospital was open that month. Tracked over time, these numbers will give you a clear picture of how well your year is progressing, businesswise.

	MON	TUE	WED	THU	FRI		MON	TUE	WED	THU	FRI
DATE	1	2	3	4	5		8	9	10	11	12
# OF DAYS	1	2	3	H	H		4	5	6	7	8
$$ PRODUCED											
$$ COLLECTED											
$$ DIFFERENCE											
# OF TRANSACTIONS											
$$ PER TRANSACTION											
# OF NEW CLIENTS											
# OF REFERRALS											
# OF NEUTERS											
# OF DENTALS											
# OF PHYSICAL EXAMS											
# OF VACCINATIONS											

Line graphs give you a more visual display of your most important numbers. One of the disadvantages of a grid is that all of the numbers begin to blend together, making it difficult to tell exactly what is happening. That's why I relied on grids for a more complete picture and line graphs for a quick look at how we were doing. The example below shows monthly production figures for year one compared to year two, tracked separately for comparison purposes:

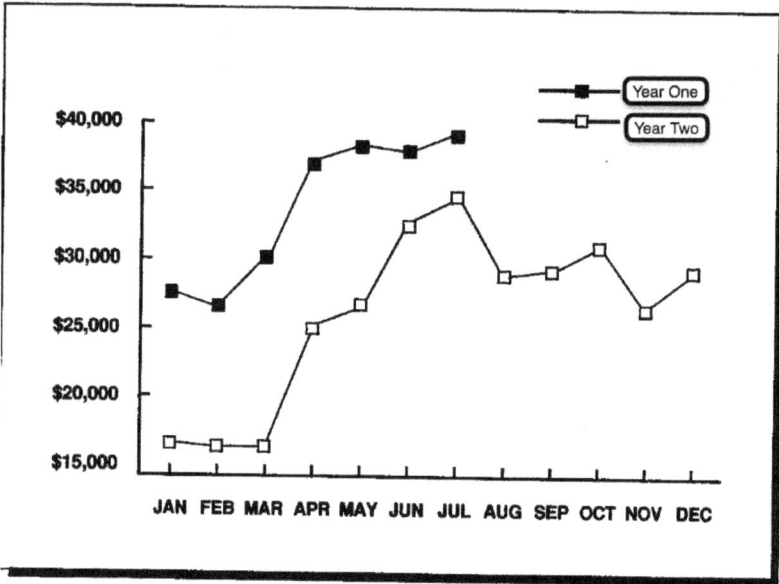

• **Bar Charts** are another option. The graph shows the month's goals right next to the actual figures that are added in week by week. Every month, we reviewed the other scoreboards, chose areas in which we wanted to improve, then tracked our goals and our progress on a bar chart. Although we didn't make our targets each month, we never failed to make a significant difference in the areas we tracked.

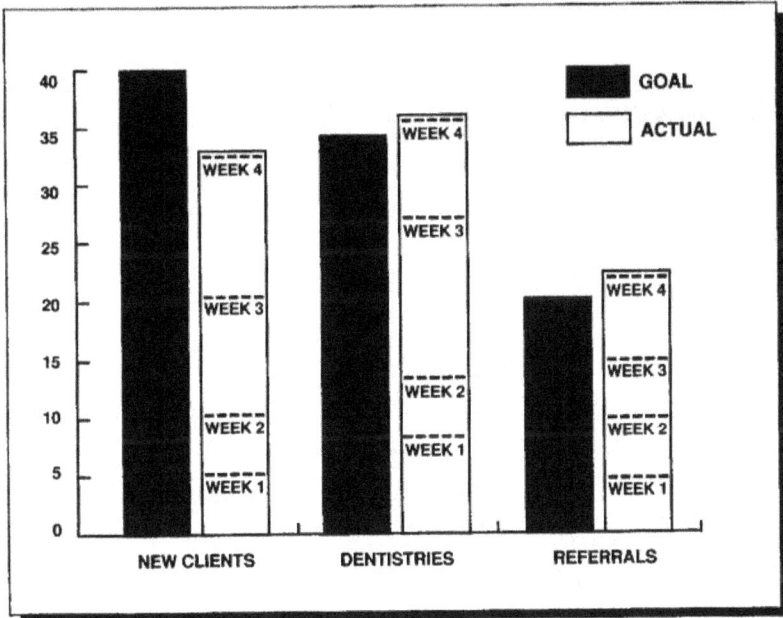

• **Pie charts** are particularly useful for summary reports, and are often clearer than a profit-and-loss statement. The example below illustrates how a pie chart on expenses can help you visualize where you're spending money—and how much remains as profit.

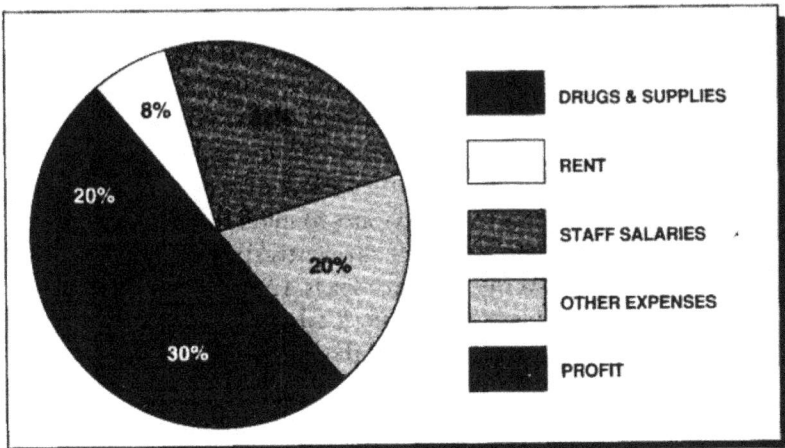

Keeping score

Developing your own system for keeping score probably sounds like a lot of work. It is. It's also the type of work that can lead to increased profits and less stress after the system is in place. How? By giving you a firm handle on how your practice is performing and what actions need to be taken to improve your performance. Here are a few suggestions for a smooth transition into scorekeeping:

1. **Start small.** Don't try to capture every conceivable number at once, or it can lead to a "statistical overdose." Begin by tracking the basic numbers on a grid with four to six headings, or on a line graph of one or two items. When you and your staff are comfortable with these basics, you can add and refine.

2. **Designate a primary scorekeeper.** I suggest it not be you. Select a dependable employee who has access to the numbers and is used to dealing with them. To reinforce the importance of the task, share this chapter with the designated scorekeeper.

3. **Involve your entire team.** After you and the primary scorekeeper set up a preliminary system, share your plan with the staff. Doing so will ensure that the time and energy invested will reap the desired rewards.

On to victory!

You're in the last two minutes of the game again. You look up at the scoreboard. Your team is behind by only three points. A couple of quick baskets would win it. You plan your strategy on the sidelines, then pull your team together for a final word. Everyone knows what you expect of them. You break from the huddle with a shout of encouragement.

Your receptionist breaks for the phones to remind clients of their annual visits. Your technicians go for the dentistries, while you and your surgery tech scrub up for the last three spays. On the final day of the month, you have your highest day ever. It takes you over the top. You win! The crowd roars...all the way to the bank.

EXERCISE

Develop two scoreboards that will give you current visual information on your practice's financial condition:

1. Does each scoreboard tell you what's happening in your business right now?

2. Is each one informative and easy to read?

3. Would other displays be more useful?

4. Which scoreboards are best suited for your entire team?

Notes:

CHAPTER 5

<<<<<<<<>>>>>>>

Superstitions That Hurt Your Business

Myths about clients, employees, and finances can paralyze your business. Isn't it time you learned the truth?

People who believe black cats are unlucky will go out of their way to avoid them. Those who don't believe in such superstitions, however, won't hesitate to pet the furry feline at their feet. Superstitions have little power over people who don't buy into them.

The veterinary profession, like any other profession or business, has its share of myths and superstitions — commonly held "truths" that affect how we run our businesses. For instance, below are some examples of common myths in the veterinary profession. Do any of these sound like similar superstitions you have in your field?

- *Breeders and dog handlers are more difficult to deal with than the average client.*
- *If another veterinary hospital moves in down the street from me, it will adversely affect my business.*
- *I'll lose clients if I raise my fees.*
- *If I want anything done right, I have to do it myself.*
- *I have to let some clients charge or they'll go elsewhere.*

This chapter will explore just how detrimental these superstitions can be to your business.

Discovering what's wrong

September was the slowest month of the year in my practice. But even though I anticipated that outcome every year—and every year proved me right—I still got upset. I knew *why* September was slow. School started in our area and parents were busy with their kids and didn't have time to worry about their pets. The most solid evidence I had was all the Septembers of the past. Until I hired my coach, Judy Billman, I never even considered the possibility that my belief could become a self fulfilling prophecy.

When Judy asked me for the facts on why we didn't do so well in September, I said, "Well, September is a slow month because . . ."

"No, that's your assessment of the month," Judy replied before I could finish. "What are the facts?"

It took me awhile to understand what she was asking, but I finally realized Judy wanted to know how much we'd billed and collected in September, how many clients we'd seen during the month, and so on. While it was true that something was different about September—our income was lower and we saw fewer clients—it wasn't because of the reasons I thought.

Putting superstitions to rest

When we investigated why we'd been slow in September for years, we learned some interesting facts: Gross income averaged about $3,000 less during September than it did in August. But when I checked with other veterinary practices around the state, I learned that September is as good a month as any other for many practitioners. I also discovered that the children in my area start school in mid-August—my busiest month.

With a little more digging, my employees and I discovered that we averaged three fewer daily client transactions in September than in other months. Over 21 working days, that meant 63 fewer client transactions. At about $45 per transaction, we were down about $3,000 in gross income. We had discovered the loss, but we were no longer willing to believe "September" was the reason.

A new approach

By investigating our superstitions and pinpointing the problems, my team and I began to realize that we were creating the situation ourselves by believing the myth and by:
- Not following up our reminder cards with a phone call, as we usually do
- Not asking clients to refer their friends to us
- Not checking the records to be sure that all of our patients were current on their routine preventive care
- Not checking teeth of every pet that came into the clinic.
  No wonder September was a slow month!

Our investigative work taught us to be on the look out for such excuses. You can follow the same approach to uncover and dispel the superstitions gripping your business?

If you think you don't have any myths to confront, take a closer look at what you hold to be true about your business — whether it's about clients, your employees, finances, or the way you think about your business. Being able to distinction between reality and superstition gives you the power and opportunity to chart your own course with effective actions — and escape superstitions that can paralyze your team.

EXERCISE

Identify the superstitions hiding in your practice:

1. Write down as many superstitions as you can. Think of any general beliefs that can't be backed up with facts. Some examples: *My staff always comes in late,* or *My clients won't pay on time,* or *No one takes any responsibility around here.* You know you've hit upon a superstition when you can add "and that's not the way it should be" to the end of it: *September is a slow month—and it shouldn't be.*

2. Choose one superstition and distinguish fact from fantasy. Be on the lookout for erroneous beliefs that have become self-fulfilling prophecies.

3. After you've gathered all the facts, explore what you and your staff can do to change the false belief.

CHAPTER 6

<<<<<<<<>>>>>>>>

Turning Business Breakdowns into Breakthroughs

No matter how hard you try to avoid them, problems in business are inevitable. So why not convert your troubles to triumphs?

We've all had days when nothing goes right—you know the kind. You start the day by walking into your office with a spring in your step and a smile on your face, only to be met with a note on your desk saying that one of your key employees has gone to the emergency room with cat-scratch fever. She won't be at work, but her attorney will be in touch. Then you open the door to your waiting room and find pandemonium. Before you can do anything, three emergency cases storm the hospital, each demanding your immediate attention.

The spring in your step falters—not to mention your smile—when your technician rushes in to tell you the X-ray machine just exploded. Not to worry, she says, no one was seriously injured. You tell her you'll be there in a moment to assess the damage, but in the meantime, to call the repair technician.

As you pass the receptionist's desk on the way to the exam room, you look at the appointment book and see that you have a full morning of exams—starting in 10 minutes. You also notice that your new receptionist has booked six grooming appointments. *Good for her*, you think—then realize the groomer isn't scheduled to come in today.

In between appointments, you rush to the staff lounge for a cup of coffee, when your long-time receptionist stops you in the hallway. *Bless her heart, here's someone I can count on*, you think. She smiles and says she has good news. *Great*, you think, *I can sure use some of that*. The news: She's three months pregnant—and she's decided not to return to work after the baby is born.

As you walk into the lounge, seriously considering adding a double shot of whiskey to your coffee, you think, *This can't be happening to me. It's just not fair to have so many problems.*

What can you do?

The above scenario may be a bit extreme, but think about how you typically react to the day-to-day problems in your business. Are you as effective at solving crises as you'd like to be? Have you ever caught yourself thinking, *If there weren't so many problems in my business, I could enjoy it more,* or *When will I ever get the practice running so smoothly there won't be any more problems?* But if spend all your time wishing there were no problems, your natural reaction to them is to get upset—and that's when you're least prepared to handle them effectively.

I believe the solution lies in accepting problems as an inevitable part of business. Although it may sound simple to do, it's not as easy to change your mindset as you might think. After all, most of us have spent years hoping all of our problems will just disappear.

Windows of opportunity

What worked for me was to accept the premise that problems are a natural part of business. It was then possible for me to start looking for "breakdowns"—interruptions that keep you from fulfilling a commitment to your clients, my staff, or myself. The next step is to turn the breakdowns into breakthroughs. Here's how:

1. Rename the problem by calling it a "breakdown." Doing so accomplishes two important goals: It makes you stop and think about what's "breaking down" in your business, and it reveals that you or your employees have been stopped in a commitment somewhere along the way. For instance, if your car gets a flat tire on the way to an important meeting, that's a breakdown. The flat prevents you from fulfilling your commitment of arriving at the meeting on time.

Another example of a breakdown: when your new receptionist books six grooming appointments on the groomer's day off. I discovered, however, that by calling the resulting dilemma a "breakdown"—then bringing the commitment to the forefront— in a better position to come up with a solution.

2. Decide what commitment the breakdown has hampered. The idea here is to shift your focus from the breakdown to the commitment you've made. Doing so will defuse the situation and make it easier for you to resolve the problem.

To show you what I mean, let's return to the example of the six grooming appointments and no groomer. Here are some of the commitments thwarted in this scenario:

• Your commitment to provide high-quality service to all

of your clients;
- Your commitment to have well-trained employees in every position;
- Your commitment to generate revenue to support the practice and your family.

3. Explore possible solutions to the breakdown. This step can be particularly effective if you ask your staff to help you brainstorm. Write down as many ideas as you can in, say, five to 30 minutes, depending on the severity of the breakdown. At this point, don't analyze the merits of each solution—just get all the possibilities out in the open. For example, to resolve the problem of not having a groomer scheduled, you could:

a. Call your groomer and ask if she could come in. You might offer additional compensation for the inconvenience.

b. Call the six clients to reschedule the grooming appointments, and explain why. To thank them for their willingness to change appointments, you could reduce their grooming fees.

c. Call a temporary agency and hire a groomer for the day.

d. Ask another employee to handle the grooming appointments. You might discover someone with hidden grooming talents in the process.

4. Choose the action that will most quickly help you fulfill your commitment and determine the resources you'll need to do so. For example, who can help you resolve the breakdown? To whom can you delegate specific tasks?

Let's say you decide to act on three of the above possibilities, beginning with "d." The first step is to call a quick meeting to see if someone on your staff can handle the grooming appointments for the day. If not, your next choice is "c": Ask your receptionist to call four or five temporary agencies for a groomer. If that doesn't work, you might try step "a": Ask an employee to find out if your groomer can come in for those six appointments.

5. Take action immediately. Start implementing the solution you've chosen by delegating specific tasks to your staff, and be sure to specify deadlines for completion. Here's an example for the grooming-appointment dilemma: "Alice, I want you to call the top five temporary agencies in the phone book and find out if they can supply a groomer today and, if so, how much it will cost. Please give me your report by 10 a.m."

You may not be used to making such bold requests. But after your staff gets accustomed to reacting quickly to resolve day-to-day breakdowns in this manner, they're likely to make plenty of their own breakthroughs.

Keep in mind that you may hit an occasional snag while trying to resolve a breakdown in your business. If so, that's simply a sign that you need to rename the problem and start the process again.

From trouble to triumph

The management technique I've outlined moves a stopped commitment forward quickly and effectively. But like anything else, the process takes practice to make it work.

After you've followed the five steps to solve breakdowns in your business, be on the lookout for other areas in your business ripe for a breakdown. You don't have to wait for problems to surface on their own. You can discover them— then solve them—anytime.

Let's say your business is cruising along fine, but you're not seeing substantial increases in production or profitability. By declaring a breakdown, then taking the five steps to overcome it, you can boost your business to the next level in a relatively short period of time.

In fact, while running my own busy practice, I learned that creating my own business breakdowns made it possible for me to handle the small problems of daily business life in a calmer, more routine fashion. And as I began to see that I *could* transform business problems into opportunities for success and growth, I realized how much more fun and rewarding my business could be.

EXERCISE

Make a list of the problems you currently face in practice and resolve one of them through the breakdown process:

1. Rename the problem by calling it a breakdown.

2. Decide what commitment the breakdown has hampered.

3. Explore solutions to the breakdown.

4. Choose the action that will most quickly help you fulfill your commitment and determine the resources you'll need to do so.

5. Take the action immediately.

Remember, the more you practice turning breakdowns into breakthroughs, the more satisfaction you'll get from your career.

CHAPTER 7

Huddle Up!

An effective staff meeting gives you the perfect opportunity to coach your team, clear the air, and boost productivity.

Your favorite basketball team is playing its arch rival. At the end of the first half, the buzzer sounds and the two teams run off the court. As you watch from the stands, the coach and his assistant stroll over to the timekeeper while his team circles around the water cooler. In a few minutes, the referee blows his whistle and the two teams walk back to center court.

What, no locker-room pep talk? you think. *Not even a huddle? What's going on?* You glance at the scoreboard to confirm that your team is behind by six points. How can they expect to come back in the second half and win the game without coaching?

Every team needs a huddle

Now think about your own game in business. When was the last time you coached your team? If you're wondering why you're coming up short each month on your scoreboard, why employees circulate through your practice like a revolving door, or why your staff is always complaining, maybe it's time to call a time-out—with a staff meeting.

I know what you're thinking. For many of you, staff

meetings simply don't live up to your expectations. In working with hundreds of small-business owners and other professionals, I've found that for most, staff meetings are difficult to schedule, disorganized, time-consuming, and unproductive. Even those who do manage to hold staff meetings often find that employees arrive in body, but not in spirit.

But what if I told you that your staff meetings could increase your business by 15 to 20 percent—or more? And what if each meeting inspired you and your staff, and gave you an action plan for making the next month extraordinary?

Give meetings another chance

In my early years of veterinary ownership, I hated staff meetings. For starters, they were impossible to schedule. When I finally did manage to get one on the calendar, it was a disaster. I finally stopped scheduling them—and no one complained. It took me years before I had the courage to try again.

When I did, I got an unexpected surprise. With the help from my business coach and plenty of trial and error, I began to learn how to lead powerful meetings that improved the quality of my practice. Huddling up with my team allowed me:

• **To clear the air.** In the course of running a busy business, tempers flare, cross words spoken, and feelings get hurt. Left unresolved, such matters can eat the heart out of the most successful team and even cause valuable employees to leave. Staff meetings give everyone an opportunity to resolve conflicts *before* a blow-up occurs.

• **To acknowledge and appreciate team players.** In

business, employees' contributions often go unrecognized. Regular staff meetings are the perfect place to acknowledge hard work, both individually and collectively. Complimenting an employee publicly can be an effective way to inspire peak performance. It also helps to smooth employee relations when staff members acknowledge each other. Remember, no contribution is too insignificant to be recognized.

• **To check the score.** It's often tough to look at the scoreboard in the middle of the game. Calling a staff meeting gives everyone a chance to catch their breath and check the score. Are you winning the game—or falling short? Meetings also allow employees to evaluate their own performance and to make sure the results are in line with the business' goals.

• **To adjust the game plan.** Staff meetings give you time to coach your players. Perhaps your employees have strayed from the game plan or you need to adjust your strategy. It's better to know where you stand at half time than after the final buzzer.

Try these tips

Effective staff meetings begin with a commitment to producing them. Before we could hold such meetings in my practice, I had to understand that all of the bad meetings in the past didn't mean future ones had be the same. I also realized that just as I could never spay a dog without being trained, I couldn't expect to lead effective meetings without learning how. Here are some of the strategies I learned that worked particularly well:

1. Identify the purpose of the meeting. In one or two sentences, summarize what objectives you intend to accomplish. Doing so gives the meeting direction and helps keep everyone on track.

2. Plan ahead. Never walk into a meeting without specifics on what you want to achieve, what issues need to be addressed, and who needs to attend. Provide a copy of the agenda prior to the meeting so that the participants have time to prepare.

Another point to consider: Unnecessary staff meetings only make the important ones more difficult, so make sure a meeting is the best way to achieve your stated purpose. Talking with an employee or sending a memo may be all that's necessary to achieve the desired result.

3. Start and end on time. Establish a clear time frame for the meeting and stick to it. Employees hate coming to a meeting on time, only to wait 15 minutes for latecomers, or attending a meeting that runs over by 30 minutes. Stress the importance of being on time to everyone invited.

4. Involve others. Don't try to lead the meeting on your own. Such gatherings are much more productive if three people take charge: one person to lead the meeting, another to record the minutes, and a third to make sure the meeting stays on track.

5. End with a specific action plan. Reserve the last quarter of the meeting for developing an action plan that includes: a) what actions need to be taken, b) who will take them, and c) when the actions should be completed. This step alone turned my staff meetings into productive, powerful sessions.

6. Decide when and with whom to have meetings.
You're the best judge of when to meet and how often. As you
plan, remember that successful meetings start with a
commitment. If you commit to one staff meeting a month for
the next six months and apply the principles, I think you'll
find that the meetings aren't that difficult to schedule.

Also keep in mind that not every employee needs to
attend every meeting. For example, if the purpose of a
meeting is to increase the number of annual check-ups and
routine vaccinations coming from your reminder system,
you may need to meet only with your front-office personnel.
If the meeting includes the entire staff, consider holding it
outside the hospital after hours. To build team spirit, you
may want to include dinner or time for socializing before the
meetings. Such occasions can be well worth the time and
money invested.

Meetings do make a difference

In my practice, I went from avoiding staff meetings at all
costs to scheduling them on a regular basis—and looking
forward to them. In fact, when we started meeting every
morning for 15 or 20 minutes to be sure everyone was ready
to play their best, my practice became more enjoyable and
productive than it had ever been. It still wasn't always easy
to find the time to get together, but we did notice the adverse
effects when we slacked off.

Staff meetings gave my team the chance to rally back
when we were slipping—just like a basketball team that's
down at the half and emerges from the locker room to go on
and win the game. Now *that's* a powerful meeting!

EXERCISE

Schedule a staff meeting in the next few weeks:

1. State the purpose of the meeting in one or two sentences.

2. Schedule the meeting with a specific time and date, and set it up far enough in advance so that employees can adjust their schedules.

3. Appoint two or three staff members to help you conduct the meeting. It's OK to lead the meeting yourself—just be sure someone else takes notes and sees to it that the meeting doesn't stray from its purpose or timeline.

4. Think about the desired outcome—before the meeting. Keep your eye on that target and make sure it includes specific, measurable results.

5. A day or two after the meeting, ask your employees what worked and what didn't. What would make the next meeting even more poductive?

6. Don't forget to include a little fun in the meetings. Holding a contest for the most creative ideas or sponsoring a raffle are good ways to generate enthusiasm and strengthen team spirit.

CHAPTER 8

<<<<<<<<>>>>>>>>

A Team in Training

A well-designed training program keeps your employees in top shape—and gives your business a competitive edge.

Winning teams practice and practice, then practice some more. For your employees to be a success, they need regular practice as well—through training. A well-designed training program will not only improve client relations, boost profitability, and strengthen staff morale, it will invigorate your business. And that's just the adrenaline rush your team needs.

A customized training regimen

An excellent way to devise an employee training program is to first determine what's missing in your business. What guidance could you provide that would significantly improve staff performance? Approaching training from this perspective is much more empowering than trying to fix what's wrong. It's a subtle yet powerful change in viewpoint—like seeing a glass of water half full *vs.* half empty. Your employees will mirror your attitude toward training, so it's important to approach the endeavor with enthusiasm.

The earlier you involve your employees in developing the training program, the more eager they'll be. Most people like to learn new things when they don't fear it's going to be shoved down their throats.

Here are three ways to approach the training:

1. General: Look for skills that are missing in your business overall and incorporate those areas into a training program for all employees. Be sure to scrutinize communication skills and business routines that everyone should know.

For instance, you may find that staff members need to brush up on their telephone skills or learn how to ask clients for referrals. Further investigation may reveal that teaching your employees how to educate clients on products and services of your business would make a real difference in productivity and sales.

2. Specific: Examine each department or position in the business for individual needs and improvements. You could start with the receptionists, then administration, then customer service, then sales staff, and finally the executives. Perhaps your receptionists need to specific communication skills. Or you may decide to enroll the specific staff members in communications skills to improve customer sales and productivity.

3. Combination: Identify both general and individual needs in your business. A combination approach can keep you from overlooking areas in need of improvement. If you decide that a large-scale training program is needed to greatly enhance your staff's skills, be sure to break the program into smaller projects spread out over time to make the most of the program and produce results.

What resources do you need?

Look for training options that will help your staff achieve specific and measurable results. Some training resources may be right under your nose. Say you have an employee who's proficient in a skill you want the rest of the staff to learn. Why not ask the staff member to hold a training session after hours? In-house training not only is convenient, it saves you money.

Your clients may be another resource: Do you know an expert who can train your staff in a specialized skill such as communication or problem solving? Perhaps they'd be willing to share their knowledge with your staff if they received a discount on future services or products.

Other training resources to consider include continuing-education classes, seminars and workshops, and audio- and video training programs. You also could team up with another business and bring in experts for a one- or two-day seminar. You'd get the advantage of a personalized meeting while sharing the cost.

As you look at your options, keep in mind that training is like any other investment: You must be willing to put in a little money if you hope to get anything out of it.

Lights, action, training!

After you've determined which resources will provide the most useful guidance, schedule the training session and assign employees to be accountable for each step of the project. While you or your manager will be ultimately responsible for the program's success, placing staff members in charge of various tasks solidifies their commitment.

Let's say your training program includes a project called

"Improving Phone Communication Skills." You put your receptionist, Sue—who's already great on the telephone—in charge of the project. Then the two of you determine the action steps needed to produce the desired results: a 20 to 30 percent increase in the number of phone shoppers who book appointment. After considering your options, you decide Sue is the best candidate to train the other receptionist. She immediately starts to prepare for an   hour-long training session for after work next week.

You may need to do a little research before the training session to determine where your business stands in a given area. For example, if you learn that only one out of 20 calls from a phone shopper results in an appointment, you know that additional training in this area could make a significant difference in the bottom line. So you set a goal to book one of every five calls from a phone shopper. Don't be afraid to set your goals high. Make it worth everyone's time to participate.

Finally, make sure your staff knows you'll monitor the results of the training. As the saying goes, always inspect what you expect. When your employees understand that you expect them to produce agreed-upon results, they'll show up for work with a good attitude—or they won't show up at all. In either case, they've done you a favor.

Other rewards count, too

I recommend that you reward employees in some way for their participation. You could give overtime pay for the time they spend in training, monetary bonuses after they've achieved the desired results, or a graduation celebration at the completion of the program.

And don't forget the fun factor. Spend some time

thinking about ways to make the learning enjoyable and ask your employees to offer their suggestions as well. Accomplishing your training goals and having a good time is a hard-to-beat combination.

EXERCISE

Schedule an hour or two to assess what's missing in your practice:

1. Determine what training would significantly improve their day-to-day performance, then ask employees for their assistance.

2. Design a staff-training program that will meet your needs. Be sure to divide an extensive program into manageable projects.

3. Present the program at a future staff meeting, and assign specific tasks to each employee.

4. Monitor the results of the training. Did the program accomplish the stated objectives? What would make the training even more effective?

Notes:

CHAPTER 9

<<<<<<<<<>>>>>>>>

You Gotta Have Heart!

Having fun at work can do wonders for productivity. Here's how to build a business with heart and soul.

Professionalism gets drilled into veterinarians early in their careers. I remember a convocation during my senior year that was devoted to, believe it or not, neckties. It's true. Apparently, a few rambunctious students had relaxed the dress code, which stipulated that all male students wear ties. "You do have a choice," the dean said with a crafty smile. "Your choice is what color tie you'll wear. But you *will* wear a tie every day."

I took his dictum to heart. After all, I was a professional— soon to be a Doctor of Veterinary Medicine. By graduation, a narrow definition of professionalism had lodged itself in my mind, and I was well on my way to being quite untouchable.

As a recent graduate, I studied my colleagues and continued to hone my professional air. By the time I purchased my own practice, I'd placed myself so high on the pedestal of professionalism, it's a wonder my nose didn't bleed. To make matters worse, my manner soon turned my practice into a brittle, boring place. Even I didn't look forward to working there, and my poor employees were wilting on the vine.

Sound familiar? I certainly hope you haven't taken the art of professionalism to such a ridiculous extreme. I'm not saying we shouldn't conduct ourselves in a dignified manner, but perhaps we can find common ground between these two extremes of professionalism.

After all, whether you're an associate, partner, sole doctor or small business owner, you're the heart and soul of it. And the higher up you go in management, the more you influence the workplace atmosphere. When I finally realized I didn't enjoy my work environment, I had to admit I had created it. Fortunately, I also was the one who could change it.

Loosen up and lighten up!

Below you'll find three proven methods to warm a practice that has become chilled too much professionalism:

1. Relax and be yourself. You may be thinking, "But as the business owner or doctor of my practice, my clients expect me to be professional." While that may be true, moderation is key. One of the most common complaints I heard from pet owners when I owned my practice was how unapproachable their veterinarian is.

But how do you go about loosening up? You can start by sharing yourself with your staff. When was the last time you told a few employees about what you did over the weekend, or related a short anecdote about your home life, or revealed a little something about your other goals and aspirations outside of work? That's sharing yourself—letting down the barriers. Sure, it's risky. Your staff may not respond as you'd hoped.

In fact, don't be surprised if your employees give you curious looks when you start to share your feelings. After all, they've known you as the tight-lipped Dr. So-and-So. When I first began to let my staff see that I was a human being, they didn't know what to make of me. I think some of the employees who'd been with me the longest had made up their minds that I wasn't human. It took awhile for them to feel relaxed around the "new me," but when they did, guess what happened? They started telling me about themselves.

My receptionist would come in after her weekend, dying to tell me about her husband's golf tournament, and I'd share about my new sport, sky diving. She couldn't believe that "her Dr. Swift" was actually jumping out of perfectly safe planes. Our exchange made us both seem more human. We did have lives outside the practice.

Don't get upset if you're not very good at opening up at first. Like anything else, it comes with practice. Most people find that when they start letting down their guard, one of two things happens: They don't know what to share, or they don't know when to stop sharing. Don't worry about it. Just do the best you can each time.

Another way to open up is to "tell one on yourself." Tell your staff about a time when you didn't look so good, a silly mistake you made, or an embarrassing moment. This approach is especially effective if you tend to be a bit too high on your professional pedestal or if, like me, you have a self-righteous attitude. By telling one on yourself, you allow the other person to relate as one human being to another.

2. Appreciate and acknowledge your team. In the busy pace of a veterinary practice, it's easy to forget to appreciate those who work with us. When I finally took the time to really look at my staff, I saw that I was surrounded by extraordinary people. What was most amazing about them is that they'd hung in there with me when I hadn't made it easy for them. They were starved for acknowledgment and didn't even realize it.

So I decided to start an Appreciation and Acknowledgment Campaign. I took a stack of paper and wrote the name of a staff member on each sheet. Then I wrote what I most appreciated about every person.

You can do the same. Perhaps your technician is always available for those late-night emergencies. Your receptionist has a beautiful smile, is always punctual, and has a flawless attendance record. Your groomer has a wonderful sense of humor and is gentle with pets. Jot down your immediate thoughts, then add to the list for the next week.

Now think about times and places to acknowledge your staff publicly—or throw an acknowledgment party. Some people may find it difficult to be in the spotlight, but don't let that stop you from acknowledging them. Believe me, your employees will get used to it—and start acknowledging each other and you.

3. Make humor and play a priority. I stood in the waiting room, feeling a little silly with a furry Koala bear puppet on my hand. It was almost closing time on a Friday afternoon, and I was clowning around with the staff after a hectic week. I thought we were finished seeing clients for the day when in walked a young couple with their new puppy.

I stood there red-faced for several seconds, my hand still inside the puppet, my staff fighting to rearrange their faces into professionals masks. Finally I nodded to the confused couple and smiled. "Don't mind me," I said with a straight face. "I just lost my thermometer, and I'm trying to find it." As I took refuge in my office, I heard my receptionist explain to the new clients that I was really a very competent veterinarian, just a little overworked lately.

Laughter and play can go a long way in warming the

coldest practice, reducing stress, and building comradery. What's more, humor is good for our bodies. In 1991, William Fry, professor emeritus in psychiatry at Stanford University, reported that laughter strengthens the immune system and boosts cardiovascular fitness by lowering blood pressure and heart rate.

Adding humor to the workplace doesn't mean you have to become a stand-up comic. In fact, the most effective humor isn't planned at all but is more of a way of looking at life. A lot of funny things happen in a veterinary clinic—and a lot of situations can benefit from a touch of humor.

Of course, humor also holds the power to wound. "There's laughing at and laughing with people," says Ann Swift, a psychotherapist who leads humor workshops for small businesses and corporations. (She's also my wife, which is no laughing matter.) Remember, humor that makes fun of another person, group, or culture is full of prejudice and more harmful than no humor at all.

It's OK to clown around

Let's say you've just performed an "exam" on your business and found it suffering from a severe humor deficiency. The symptoms include high-stress fever, constant turnover, staff members calling in sick at every turn, and general malaise.

To start treatment, you must first change your attitude and that of your staff. Most people are serious at work because they think that's what their employers expect of them. But if your staff begins to realize it's OK to have a little fun at work, they'll think of their own ways to add spice to the practice—and enhance the work environment in the process. Here are some ideas you can use to infuse humor into your workplace:

• Wear a red clown nose or glasses with bushy eyebrows and a large nose to work. Wait to see how long it takes someone on your staff to comment. If you go through the whole day without a word, you'll know you've got a critical case of 'serious workplace syndrome'.

• Designate a bulletin board as a "humor board." Invite everyone, including your clients, to bring in their favorite jokes, cartoons, or funny anecdotes.

• Turn part of your staff lounge into a "humor corner" where staff members can go on their breaks. Provide a set of jacks, audio tapes of your favorite comedians, Nerf balls, and so on.

• Pass out "stress support kits." Include a set of wind-up chattering teeth (great when you're on the phone with someone who's long-winded), pens that look like vegetables (the CIA once ordered 200 of them from PlayFair, Inc.), an emergency chocolate bar (for those really down moments), or a pocket mirror (to see how silly you look when you frown).

• Follow this lead: Matt Weinstein of PlayFair, Inc., says that one of his clients shut down his office for two hours one day and took his staff to the local mall, where he gave each employee $200. "This is my money," Weinstein's client said, "but you can keep whatever you buy with it in the next hour as long as it's for you." The shopping spree that followed became the major topic of conversation around the office for months.

• Build humor into your staff meetings by starting with something funny, like this quip, which The HUMOR Project's Joel Goodman quotes from Robert Frost: "The brain is a wonderful organ. It starts the moment you get up in the morning and does not stop until you get to work."

Heart and Soul

If my freeze-dried practice could be revitalized through these methods, so can yours. It *is* possible to enjoy work, appreciate those around you, and be yourself. And don't be surprised if your revenue makes a significant jump as well. After all, people work more productively in an environment where they're nurtured and appreciated. That's a practice with heart and soul.

EXERCISE

Practice raising your hospital's humor quotient:

1. Start sharing yourself with your staff. If you find it uncomfortable to talk about your personal life, try out two- to three-minute anecdotes on your family first. The stories may be funny, heartwarming, or simply interesting—the idea is to show your employees another side of you.

2. Organize an Acknowledgment and Appreciation Campaign. Make a list of your employees' contributions. What do you most appreciate about each person? What has each done beyond the call of duty?

3. Add a dose of laughter and play to work. Choose one or more of the suggestions in this chapter or make up your own. Then get your staff to join in on the planning—and the fun.

Notes:

Section

TWO

Coaching Effective Communication

CHAPTER 10

<<<<<<<<<>>>>>>>>>

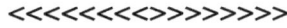

Straight Talk

To encourage clients to accept your recommendations, you must turn complicated jargon into easy-to-grasp conversation.

You know those days when you are ready to serve your customers and clients with your products and services, and yet at the end of the day many of them have left your place of business without purchasing or scheduling anything even though in your conversation they said they were ready to buy.

What's missing from such interactions is straight talk— easy-to-understand conversations that elicit your clients' agreement. I'm not talking about selling, or cajoling, or the silvery-tongue talk we've come to expect of usual hard sell salesperson. I'm talking about *enrolling* clients and customer in what they want.

As you may recall in the third semester of Communication Skills for Professionals… What? You never took any courses in communication? Exactly my point. Neither did I. It took me almost 10 years of beating my head against the wall before I started to study my communication style.

I'll continue to study the subject the rest of my life. And I have learned a few ways to manage those sales conversations that take place in all businesses. That's where straight talk can pay off—in developing stronger client relationships and in providing more services.

Don't ignore the client or customer!

You have a relationship with every client or customer you have. The relationship may go back for years. For example, I had always been Mrs. Ellis' vet and she'd never think of taking Fluff anywhere else. Or the relationship may be a new one: You've never seen Mr. Webster before, but Fluff's owner referred him. No matter what your relationship with the client, you must re-establish and strengthen that bond at every visit.

My tendency used to be to go straight for the animal with thermometer and stethoscope. Get to the physical exam, never mind the client. Unfortunately, this approach didn't work too well. Clients want to be acknowledged just like the rest of us.

I'm afraid my inclination to avoid people started early. When I was 6 years old, I switched from wanting to be a physician to a veterinarian because I didn't like to hear people complain. I figured it would be a lot easier to treat pets. It wasn't until I was a senior in veterinary school that I realized nearly 100 percent of the animals I had seen—and would continue to see during my veterinary career—all had a human being on the other end of the leash. People who not only knew how to complain about their pet's ailments as well as their own, but who held the checkbook and credit cards. If I was going to stay in business, I knew I'd better start paying more attention to the two-legged animals.

Reinforcing your long-term relationship with an established client doesn't have to be elaborate or time-consuming. It can be as simple as, "Good morning, Mrs. Ellis. It's great to see you again. Did you realize you've been bringing Fluff to me for almost 10 years—ever since she was 8 weeks old? You've been an outstanding pet owner...."

Connecting with a new client might take a bit longer, but think of the time as a good investment: "Mr. Webster, welcome to my clinic. I understand from Donna that Susan Ellis, one of our most loyal clients, recommended us to you. I want you to know how much we appreciate you giving us the opportunity to care for your dog. I hope this is the start of a long relationship, like we've had with Mrs. Ellis...."

If such conversations sound unnatural to you, try substituting your own words and personal style. Whatever you do, don't ignore the opportunity to build strong client relationships.

The client may be listening—but not to you

Have you ever noticed that we're constantly having internal conversations with ourselves? Right now, that little voice inside your head may be saying, *Am I really going to get anything out of this chapter? Can this really affect my business?* You and I listen to that voice every waking minute of the day —and it's often what keeps us awake at night. What that means for you is that just because a client appears to be listening to you, doesn't mean he or she really is. But you can bet the person is listening to an internal conversation.

Perhaps you can recall standing face to face with a client, discussing a complicated issue when you noticed a blank look on the person's face. But you didn't know what it meant, so you kept talking—only to learn that the client didn't understood a word you said? We've all been there.

Chances are, the client got hooked by his or her internal conversation, which wasn't even related to the issue. You may have said "issue" and the person suddenly remembered they were out of "tissues" at home and needed to stop at the store on the way home. Whatever the case, the client wasn't listening to you.

So what can you do about this dilemma? For starters, you can listen to your own internal conversation. That may sound like strange advice, but if you imagine what the client *might* be thinking, you'll know how to address his or her likely concerns.

Let me use an example from my own business. Discussing fees for complicated medical or surgical cases are often a real challenge. Imagine you're about to discuss the finances for complicated piece of surgery. Based on what you know about the client, you believe she's likely to hit the roof when you tell her the fee. But rather than step around the issue, you get it out in the open:

"Mrs. Burgess, I know this sounds like a complicated procedure, and it is. I've performed many of these procedures successfully in the past. Together, with me doing the surgery and you helping with the after care, I know Fefe will do just fine.

"I also want you to know what the fee for this type of surgery will because I realize money is often a factor that needs to be considered in such situations. I've done a number of these procedures before quite successfully, so I know you can expect the total fee to be in a range of from $700 to $850."

Mrs. Burgess's reaction will depend on her internal conversation about money. Most people react strongly to financial issues, but there's no formula for every situation. If you notice a shocked look on Mrs. Burgess's face, you could say something like: "I realize you probably didn't expect to have to deal with all this when you got up this morning, did you?" Instead of trying to justify the fee, let Mrs. Burgess express herself. Just getting the client to communicate her feelings does a lot to defuse a tense issue.

Give it to 'em straight

Can you recall walking into a store to buy a major appliance or piece of electronics you didn't know much about? You did fine until you started talking with a salesclerk who wanted to show you how much he knew about the item. You may have even walked out of the store empty-handed because you were too confused to know what to buy.

Now think about your clients. Isn't it possible we do the same thing to them? The problem isn't that we already know more than our clients but that we're so determined to tell them every bit of it. Straight talk means keeping things simple. No matter how complicated a situation may be, you can usually break the conversation into four steps:

1. State the problem.

2. Discuss the possible consequences of the problem if it goes unresolved.

3. Make one or more recommendations that will alleviate the problem.

4. Request that action be taken and by when.

Let's return to the example of Mr. Webster, the new client who brought in his dog for an exam. Here's what you might say for each step:

1. State the problem: "Mr. Webster, although Champ seems to be in good general health, I did find three areas of concern—her teeth, her ears, and a lump on her left leg. First, let's consider her teeth. They're not in good shape. Over the last six years Champ has built up a lot of tartar and her gums are very inflamed."

2. Discuss the possible consequences: "If we don't take

care of the problem, Champ could lose her teeth. In addition, bad teeth and gums have an adverse effect on her overall health."

3. Make your recommendation: "I recommend that we take two steps to alleviate this problem. First, let's schedule Champ to come in later this week and thoroughly clean those teeth and treat her gums. We'll clean them just like your dentist cleans your teeth, with one exception. We'll sedate Champ so that she won't feel any discomfort and so that we'll be able to do a good job.

"Second, we'll go over a home dental-care program that will help you keep Champ's teeth in good shape. Do you have any questions up to this point?" (You'd use the same approach for the pet's ear and lump problems, explaining that it would be best to treat all three problems at the same time so the pet would have to be anesthetized only once.)

4. Request action: "OK, let's get Champ scheduled. Which day later this week works best for you?" (If you prefer a more direct approach, you could say: "I'd like to see Champ back in on Thursday. How does that work for you?")

Let clients catch up

Have you ever missed a key piece of information in a joke and realized after the punch line that you'd missed the point entirely? Our clients feel this way all the time, but it's not funny. Talking over a client's head usually makes the person feel alienated—and that's not a good frame of mind to be in when making a big decision.

Suppose you walk into the exam room after getting the results of a patient's heartworm and fecal exam. "Mr. Smith,

I've got some bad news. Ol' Butch has heartworms and hookworms. Now what we'll have to do is have him come in for some bloodwork and X-rays to see if we'll be able to treat him for the heartworms. While he's here, we'll go ahead and treat him for the hookworms...." When you're finished, you wonder why Mr. Smith didn't understand anything you said.

It might be because you left him at the starting gate— back at "I've got some bad news." That little comment likely triggered Mr. Smith's fear for his pet's health—and got him listening to an internal conversation. Anything you said later got drowned out.

If Mr. Smith was able to get beyond that opener, you probably lost him when you said you needed to do X-rays to treat Ol'Butch for hookworms. Or perhaps he got confused over why Butch had to come in for tests when you were going to treat him for the worms while he was in the hospital. Have you ever notice how much "hookworms" and "heartworms" sound alike? Or how hard it is to think clearly when someone is talking fast and you're worried about the news?

Checking for understanding periodically during the conversation can help alleviate this problem. Clients get a chance to catch up and join in—and it keeps their internal conversations at bay. What's more, clients can clarify issues so that the rest of the discussion makes sense to them.

Tackle touchy issues head-on

Most of us hate confrontations of any kind, but it's not a good idea to dance around sensitive subjects. All too often such omissions just come back to haunt you. You know you've stepped over an issue that needs to be addressed if the client looks worried or irritated or if you run into an uncomfortable silence.

Take Mrs. May, for example. You know from years of experience that this client is quite self-assured. When she makes the uncharacteristic excuse, "I'll have to check with my husband," you know something is up. You could ignore her comment, but chances are it will only plague you later.

A better option would be to uncover what went unsaid: "Mrs. May, I'm surprised to hear you say that. In the past, you've always made the decisions about Kallie's care. Is there something you aren't saying?"

Pretty direct, right? But it's likely that such a person would appreciate your straight talk and respond in kind.

Show your appreciation

This last piece of advice is important: Always acknowledge your clients. Unlike compliments, which often border on insincerity, acknowledgments recognize something special about a person—without sounding flowery. One example: "Mrs. Allen, I want to thank you for making your appointment on time. You know, that's something I've noticed about you. You always keep your appointments and you're never late. I really appreciate it."

If you don't think that kind of talk makes a big difference to clients, wait until the next time someone acknowledges you and see how good it feels. What's more, doesn't it make you feel good about the person who did the acknowledging?

Where to go from here

This chapter could end up as an interesting discussion that makes little difference in your relationships—or it could lead to major changes. The outcome depends on whether you put the suggestions to work. Are you willing to change how you talk with others? If so, I suggest you start by practicing on your staff.

It's especially important to acknowledge others. But instead of telling your staff you want to practice that skill, just do it and gauge the results. If you're team is like mine, they won't know what's going on and may even be suspicious at first. Don't worry. Keep it up and they'll come to love it.

When you're comfortable with such talk, try it on your clients. Clear, concise, and complete communication may not convince every client to accept every recommendation, but it will boost the percentage of agreement dramatically. Even clients who refuse to comply will understand why you recommended what you did, and they'll know it's up to them to say yes or no. And so will you.

EXERCISE

Meet with your staff to practice exam-room conversations:

1. Think of the conditions you commonly see in your business, and ask staff members to name the problems they see most often as well. Employees who don't have such conversations with customers can pose as clients.

2. Listen to your staff as they go through a mock dialogue, then coach them on how to make the exchange even better. Be sure to first point out what worked well in each conversation, followed by what could make it even better.

3. Be sure your staff makes recommendations that are consistent with your business philosophy and that a consultation may be necessary.

4. Ask your imaginary clients to take a specific action within a certain period of time. Help your employees practice this step until everyone can make such requests confidently.

Notes:

CHAPTER 11

<<<<<<<<>>>>>>>

Tell Your Staff to Speak UP!

Your employees need to know that if they bring their concerns to you, you'll listen closely, really hear them—and work with them find solutions.

This chapter examines an insidious disease that often goes undiagnosed. Instead of affecting patients, however, the disease attacks your business. I call it "constipated communication" and it manifests itself when you or a staff member can't speak freely for fear of reprisal. Some common excuses: *Oh, well, it really isn't important, or I couldn't say that to him, or I'll clear up the problem later*—but no one ever does. Before long, what isn't being said is running your practice.

I've found that stuck communication occurs in almost every business to one degree or another, yet it often remains hidden except in the most terminal cases. After one veterinarian diagnosed the condition in his clinic, he said, "It's like going through your entire life constipated, so you think constipation is the way it is supposed to be." Although jammed communication may not kill your practice, it will certainly keep it from thriving.

Symptoms that sabotage?

When I performed a "physical" on my practice, I found symptoms of constipated communication. As you read the list, think about your own business:

• **Gossip.** Is your business growing a well-tended grapevine? If you tell an employee something in confidence, does your receptionist know about it before you get back up front? Do you find yourself excusing this symptom like I did by saying, "But people gossip in all businesses"?

• **Complaining.** If you were to step outside your practice for a moment and listen to the conversations inside, what would you hear? In a constipated business, you'll hear a lot of complaining, especially when the owner isn't around. Have you ever walked into a room and noticed that everyone suddenly stopped talking? Do people complain to those who can do nothing about the problem?

I consulted with one veterinary practice employed a master complainer. He dominated people with his complaining, yet he also had an important position in the hospital and did his work well. After diagnosing constipated communication in that hospital, we realized that the employee was trying to express his desire to be a leader in the practice. He wanted power and the only way he knew to get it was by complaining louder and longer than anyone else.

• **Covert communication.** This symptom is one of the most common in a business with stuck communication and yet it is one of the most difficult to detect. If people don't feel they can express their feelings, you can be sure they'll find another way to "say" it.

For instance, do some of your employees show up 10 or 15 minutes late for work regularly? Or does a seemly healthy employee call in sick a lot, especially when you are the busiest? Do you find that about the time you get someone trained, he or she leaves to work at a hospital down the street—but doesn't tell you why? Do new employees start out highly motivated but within a few weeks they start doing just enough to get by?

If your staff doesn't feel it's OK to say what they feel, they'll find other ways to communicate their feelings. In the worst-case scenario, the people express their frustration by treating customers and clients rudely.

'It's all their fault'

Practice owners who discover they own a constipated practice tend to respond this way: "Well, it's their fault they didn't talk to me if they had a problem. My door is always open to them, but no one ever comes to me. They never let me know what's on their mind."

I said the same thing in my practice: "Feel free to come in my office and talk to me about anything that's on your mind." But my actions contradicted that message. If an employee came to me with a complaint, I'd yell at them, or I'd drag in the employees they were complaining about and yell at all of them. "Don't ever do it again," I'd say—and they never would. They'd never again make the mistake of coming to me with a problem.

If an employee made a suggestion to improve the business, I'd do one of two things: I'd immediately give all the reasons the idea wouldn't work, or I'd tell the person "I'll think it over."— and then never say another word about it. In spite of my open-door policy, my actions clearly said: "Don't bother me? You'll either get yelled at or ignored."

It took my coach, Judy Billman, to point out the mixed message. Once I realized such behavior was a clear sign of constipated communication, I knew I had to assume responsibility for treating it. To unclog my practice I began to adopt this principle: "I am responsible for everything that occurs in my practice—both good and bad."

Four steps to a new you

I realized that the only way to improve my communication skills would be to analyze how I communicate. I started asking myself some tough questions. Although the exercise didn't offer a quick fix, it did open my mind—and gave me a whole new way of communicating with others. As I went about my business each week, I worked on a different question:

1. How often do I shut people down, verbally or otherwise, and keep them from saying what's on their mind? That first week I began to notice how often I interrupted people or finished their thoughts for them. Or I'd tell a staff member to see me later but never make time. Other times, my tone of voice or my posture told employees to stay away.

At the end of the week I felt sick at heart. If I wanted to open up communication in my practice, I obviously had a lot to do. If you find that you frequently shut down those around you, don't be too hard on yourself. Most people do the same thing and don't realize it.

2. What is the commitment behind every complaint? I began to see complaints for what they really are: an indication that something is interfering with an employee's ability to fulfill a commitment. My staff wouldn't bother to complain at all if they didn't feel strongly about the practice and their role in it.

For example, instead of getting angry when my

technician complained about having to cover the front desk when the receptionist was absent, I looked for the commitment behind her complaint. I learned that she was committed to educating clients about such topics as nutrition, FeLV, and pet dentistry and that covering the front desk kept her from being in the exam room.

3. What would I say to my staff if I were free to express yourself fully? This exercise was a tough one for me. I not only had to become aware of when I wasn't saying something I wanted to, but figure out what was stopping me. During the first part of the week, I kept track of what I wasn't saying and why. Then I spent the rest of the week speaking my mind. I started small and worked up.

It's a good idea to tell your staff what you're doing. If you're not comfortable sharing the information with everyone, go to a trusted staff employee and say something like, "Sally, I've noticed lately that there are times when I don't feel I can say what's on my mind without something terrible happening. I'd like to ask you a favor. For the rest of the week, I'd like to be able to say to you anything that's on my mind. I'm asking you because I know I can trust you to handle it responsibly. Will you do it?"

4. What would my staff be like if they were free to express themselves fully? I spent the fourth week observing how people act when they aren't free to be candid—and I noticed how shut down they were. But by the end of the week, I found myself beginning to open up. Although my staff didn't trust me at first, I discovered that by creating a safe space for them to communicate openly, they started to follow my lead. In turn, I didn't try solve their problems, and argue with them. I just put myself in their world.

I responded only when I was so sure of what they said that I could argue the point in their favor. We could then work on solutions to the problem together. In some cases, I took the same action I would have taken even if I hadn't gone through the process, but the results were dramatically different. Why? Because I was working with people who knew they had been heard—maybe for the first time.

Be vigilant

Constipated communication isn't a disease that can be cured once and then forgotten. If I slipped back into old habits, it didn't take long for the communication in my practice got clogged again.

I suggest you check the communication channels in your business from time to time—or you'll wake up one morning with a sick business again. One idea: Hold a staff meeting once a month and ask everyone to share any concerns and complaints.

Once we unclogged the communication in my practice, a few staff members commented on how the communication skills had improved their relationships outside of work. By that time, I wasn't surprised by the news. I'd already noticed the rewards in my own life—and you will too.

EXERCISE

Spend a month asking yourself these four communication questions:

1. How often do you shut people down, verbally or otherwise, and keep them from saying what's on their mind?

2. What is the commitment behind every staff complaint?

3. What would you say to your staff if you were free to express yourself fully?

4. What would your staff be like if they were free to express themselves fully?

Notes:

CHAPTER 12

<<<<<<<<>>>>>>>>

Turning Complaints into Gold

Staff and client complaints can be a rich resource for improving your business. It's all in how you listen.

Early one Monday morning, Dr. McGrath strolls up the sidewalk of his veterinary practice, pausing for a moment to take a deep breath of fresh air. *What a gorgeous spring day,* he thinks. As he opens the back door to his hospital, his receptionist almost runs over him as a Newfoundland drags her down the hall.

That's strange, Dr. McGrath thinks as he closes the door. *Why isn't Peter, the kennel attendant, doing that instead of Marge?* As Dr. McGrath starts toward his office to put on his lab coat, he bumps squarely into Marge, who's now on her way back from the kennel.

"What's going on?" he asks as they untangle themselves.

"That good-for-nothing Peter didn't show up for work this morning—and after a heavy boarding weekend to boot!" Marge complains. "I can't believe the nerve of some people. There must be 20 clients out front, the phone is ringing off the hook, and I slammed my knee against the filing cabinet—all because Peter decided to sleep in!"

Uh-oh, Dr. McGrath thinks, watching a red-faced Marge hurry down the hall. Where is his always-there-with-a-smile receptionist, the one with a cheerful word for the every client? Something is definitely wrong.

At 10:05, Marge hands Dr. McGrath a client's record and nods toward the exam rooms. "Mr. Cooper is in exam room 3. He's very upset about his bill and would like to speak with you," she says.

Uh-oh, Dr. McGrath thinks to himself again. *What's wrong now?* As he steps inside the room, he tries to smile pleasantly. "Hello, Mr. Cooper. What can I do for you on this lovely spring day?"

"You can explain to me where you got your license to steal me blind," Mr. Cooper snaps. "This is the most outrageous bill I've ever seen! You charged me an outrageous amount to board a teacup poodle? She doesn't eat more than three teaspoons of food a day. How could you possibly charge so much?"

Oh, boy, I've really done it this time, Dr. McGrath groans to himself. *It's going to be a long day.*

You can't hide from complaints

Everyone complains about something sometime. Unfortunately, being part of the human race also means having to listen to others when they complain. And yet the question isn't how to keep staff members, clients, or loved ones from complaining, but how to listen to what they're *really* saying.

Think about how you usually respond to complaints. If you're like many people, you automatically assume that a complaint means something is wrong—either with the person complaining, with the situation, or perhaps with yourself for giving the person reason to complain.

Whenever I heard a staff member complain in my practice, I got upset or angry, and I responded to what I perceived as something wrong. I would then pull the person into my office to have "a little talk"—which usually meant I'd lecture the employee about how damaging complaining was to staff morale. Or I'd get angry with the person for making such a fuss and demand that he or she shape up or ship out. My staff soon realized it wasn't safe to complain around me. That didn't stop them from complaining, however—they just did it behind my back.

The same was true with my clients and my family. I became quite effective at stifling communication, yet I couldn't figure out why I had such turnover of staff, clients, and yes, even loved ones.

There *is* a better way

When I realized I was hurting communication, I started rethinking my reactions. I began to understand that within every complaint is a nugget of gold—a wealth of information that if used correctly could help my practice. To mine this gold, however, I had to listen to complaints in a new way. Instead of listening for what was wrong, I began to listen for what the complaint meant—a process I call "creative listening."

For example, when Dr. McGrath heard the complaints Monday morning, he automatically assumed something was wrong—with Marge, Peter, Mr. Cooper, and himself for not being a better manager. But what if he had *really* listened and thought about what caused his staff and clients to complain in the first place?

With careful listening, Dr. McGrath would have understood that Marge is committed to the smooth flow of the practice and offering the best client service possible. More important, he would have realized that when circumstances inhibit her commitment to the practice, Marge gets upset and complains.

And what if Dr. McGrath had listened to Mr. Cooper's complaint about his boarding bill as though his long-time client had something to contribute to the practice? Instead of thinking of Mr. Cooper as a cheapskate or worrying that the boarding fee really is too high, he might have seen that perhaps Mr. Cooper simply wants to know about charges in advance. By listening creatively, Dr. McGrath also might have realized that a hospital tour to show Mr. Cooper what the boarding fee covers could further alleviate his frustration.

Practice, practice, practice

Creative listening is a skill. You may be awkward at first, but with practice you can mine gold from any conversation, no matter how loud the complaints. After you've changed your behavior, you can teach others. Here are a three suggestions:

1. Train yourself first. Spend a couple of weeks writing down each time you hear a complaint and catch yourself listening for what's wrong instead of listening creatively. This work is likely to change the way you listen, so don't be surprised if others start noticing the change in your behavior as well. When you find that the people around you are beginning to communicate their concerns to you, you're ready for the next step.

2. Train your staff. Now tell your team what you've been doing. Explain how you listened to complaints in the past and how you're trying to change old patterns. If your staff has noticed the difference in your behavior, they'll be more interested in learning from you.

3. Make a game out of creative listening. To encourage your staff to listen creatively, consider offering silly prizes to the person who collects the most complaints, the staff member who offers the best complaint, or the employee who improves his or her listening skills the most. Ask your staff to share the gold they find in their own or other's complaints. Most important, look for opportunities to acknowledge your staff when they listen creatively.

It's all in how you listen

Before you run away from another complaint, think about how you can use the information it reveals to strengthen your practice and your personal life. In fact, when you share your insights with the person complaining, you may be startled by how appreciative he or she is to know you really listened. With practice, you can turn what's often considered a negative into a wealth of opportunity.

EXERCISE

Think of the automatic way most of us listen to others as a radio station constantly playing inside your head. Like many late-night stations, "WYOU" is fully automated unless you, the program director, override the system. Your mission is to program WYOU with different "music" by listening creatively to complaints. You'll soon discover that listening this way is the quickest route to resolving sticky conversations with your team, clients, family and friends.

Write down your insights about complaining and how you will put this new way of listening to work.

CHAPTER **13**

<<<<<<<<<>>>>>>>>

Defusing Explosive Client Conversations

When tempers flare, it's up to you and your team to smooth things over and offer amends.

Millicent doesn't know it, but there's a time bomb on her desk behind the reception counter. Her best friend, Allison and coworker, unwittingly planted the bomb during her lunch break. Neither staff member knows it, but the bomb is about to explode. T minus 10 seconds and counting.

It's 5:45 p.m. on one of the more frenzied days for Five Points Veterinary Hospital. The clients are three deep on the other side of the counter. Millicent, usually one of the most efficient receptionists who ever punched a time clock, is struggling to keep up with the after-work rush. No wonder she hasn't noticed the bomb ticking. Besides, it's disguised as Andrew Hawkins' client record. T minus 5 seconds.

"I'm here to pick up Freddie. I dropped him off for a bath and dip," Mr. Hawkins says. On most any other day, Millicent's trained ear would detect the strained chord in his voice, but not today.

Without looking up, Millicent pulls Freddie's record from the discharge tray, and slides the statement toward the client. "Your total comes to $109, Mr. Hawkins," Millicent says, reading the statement upside down. As the words leave her mouth, a small voice in the back of her mind says, *Wow, that's a lot for a bath and dip.* "Will that be cash, check, or charge . . . ?" T-minus 0.

"$109?" Mr. Hawkins thunders. "You've got to be kidding! That's outrageous! All I asked for was a bath and dip. I'm not paying for anything else. Surely you don't mean a lousy bath and dip costs over a hundred bucks! What's going on? Is the doc ready to buy a new Mercedes?"

Caught off guard by Mr. Hawkins' outburst, Millicent pulls the statement back and studies the itemization. "The $109 includes Freddie's inoculations, a physical exam, and lab tests to check him for intestinal worms and heartworms," Millicent replied. Feeling attacked, she adds, "It's hospital policy. All dogs coming into the hospital must be current on their vaccinations."

That last comment is like pouring gasoline on a fire. Mr. Hawkins' face turns crimson and the veins in his neck poke out. "Blast your policies. I never authorized that treatment, and I'm not paying for it. Where's Dr. Blake? Never mind. Just get me my dog."

Sound familiar? If you've ever worked in a veterinary clinic, you and your staff have probably faced such situations more than once. Your employees, however, often suffer the brunt of these upsets because clients tend to be more demonstrative when you're not around. So what can you do to defuse the difficult conversations that blow up in everybody's face from time to time? An effective coaching technique is to find out what was missing in a given situation that would have made a difference in the outcome.

Pretend you're the client

To learn what's missing in a conversation gone awry, you must step into the client's and see the situation through his or her perspective. For example, how many times have you been waited on by someone who barely acknowledged your existence? The person never smiled, never looked you in the eyes, never said a word. If he or she did speak, the words sounded like a recorded message. That's what happened with Millicent. In the flurry of the day, she changed from a human being into a "human doing," and forgot to step into Mr. Hawkins' world. If she had, she would have realized that he'd had a terrible day. Most of his frustration wasn't even directed at Millicent. She just got in the way.

Human beings seldom get upset about just what's happening at a given moment. We're always carrying our past around—all those experiences that made us feel embarrassed, rejected, or foolish. The feelings can stem from events that occurred during early childhood or just moments before. Then, when faced with a similar experience, we get upset all over again. We're instantly catapulted back to an earlier event. You might say people are upsets, looking for a place to happen.

Perhaps you can recall a time when someone said something rather innocuous to you, but you got really upset. Over-reacting this way happens a lot, and for the most part we're unaware of what's going on. We think we're upset because of what the person said when the comment actually triggered past feelings and experiences.

You and your team will be much more effective in dealing with upsets if you remember not to take them personally. Millicent felt that Mr. Hawkins was attacking her, so she struck back, resorting to line about "the hospital's policy." I know it's hard not to take it personally when an irate client is climbing down your throat, but give it your best shot.

Partners in resolution

To defuse the situation with Mr. Hawkins, Millicent must focus not on what she should *do* in the matter, but who she will *be*. If the she remembers not to take Mr. Hawkins' upset personally, she can be there for him without feeling the need to defend herself. In other words, she can be of service to him.

If you've ever been with someone who, in spite of the fact you were upset and blasting away at the person, he or she continued to look for how to take care of you, you know how calming this response can defuse be. In Millicent's case, being of service to Mr. Hawkins may have included reassuring him that the misunderstanding could and would be resolved quickly and fairly.

It's a good idea to remove an upset client from the scene where the upset occurred. Doing so allows two things to happen: The person has an opportunity to settle down, and you don't have worry about an audience. Both parties usually appreciate a little cooling-off period.

If the client continues to be upset, let him or her vent. Most people simply want to be heard and understood. You don't have to agree or disagree with what the person is saying, just listen carefully. In fact, it's best not to side with the client or try to defend your position. Just listen in such a way that the person sees that you understand.

After the client has expressed everything he or she wanted to say to someone who's listening to understand, most of the time the upset will disappear or at least become much less intense. In some situations, listening with understanding may be all you have to do. I've had some of the most irate clients rant and rave at me while I swallowed hard and listened. When it was all over, they said, "Thanks for listening, Doc. I just needed to get that off my chest."

Once you've shown the client you're interested in being of service, and the upset has lost its energy, figure out how to best resolve the problem. In Mr. Hawkins' case, your response might go like this: "Mr. Hawkins, is there anything else you're upset about?"

"No, that's about it. I'm sorry I blew up like that, but I wasn't prepared for such a bill."

"I understand, Mr. Hawkins. Let's look and see what we can come up with together to reach a resolution. What do you feel would be fair?" Don't be surprised if the client requests far less than what you're prepared to give. If that's the case, you know you've done a good job of listening to understand.

Learning how to deal effectively with explosive client conversations takes practice. It may be helpful to remember that every time you face an angry client, you have a golden opportunity to train yourself and coach your staff to provide higher levels of client satisfaction.

EXERCISE

To respond to difficult client situations with grace, practice mock conversations with your staff.

1. Have one person be the irate client and another a staff member. To make the scenario seem real, use actual incidents as much as possible.

2. Ask the rest of the staff to listen to the mock conversation without saying anything until the end. Then debrief the mock by pointing out what worked and then what might have made the exchange even more effective.

CHAPTER 14

<<<<<<<<<>>>>>>>>

Does Your Team Get the Respect They Deserve?

They will—if you take the time to show clients how vital your employees are to your business.

Dr. Akins stood behind the receptionist's counter, checking the appointment book for the afternoon schedule. She'd returned from lunch a few minutes early and hadn't yet put on her lab coat. But before the doctor could get to her office, Mrs. Arbuckle, one of the practice's newest clients, arrived for the afternoon's first appointment.

The receptionist hadn't returned from lunch yet, so Dr. Akins decided to take care of Mrs. Arbuckle herself. Glancing at the patient record, the doctor noticed this was Mrs. Arbuckle's second visit; Siegfried, her pampered Persian, needed his second set of vaccinations. "Good afternoon, Mr. Arbuckle. How are you and Siegfried doing today?"

"We're fine," Mr. Arbuckle replied gruffly. "Good, no one else is here. Maybe this means the doctor won't keep me waiting almost 10 minutes like she did on my last visit."

Taken aback, Dr. Akins said, "I'm sorry if you had to wait last time, but I'm sure we can get you in and out in a jiffy today."

"I hope so," Mr. Arbuckle replied. "I spend a lot of good money here."

Fighting to maintain a pleasant smile, Dr. Akins decided her best strategy was to offer no reply. Obviously, Mrs. Arbuckle wasn't having a good day. The doctor led the pair into the first exam room, then excused herself.

As she passed through the waiting room, Dr. Akins approached the receptionist, who was sitting behind the counter. "Mrs. Arbuckle arrived a couple of minutes early, so I put her in Room 1. I'll warn you, she's not having a good day, so treat her with kid gloves."

"Oh, I don't think Mrs. Arbuckle has any good days," the receptionist replied. "She sure treated me rudely on her first visit."

"That's funny, I don't remember her being rude before," Dr. Akins said. She donned her stethoscope and lab coat, took a deep breath, and put on a smile as she entered the examination room.

"Oh, Dr. Akins, it's so good to see you again," Mrs. Arbuckle gushed. "Siegfried is doing so well. I think he really enjoys coming to see you." Mrs. Arbuckle's change in attitude hit Dr. Akins like a wave crashing on a beach.

A case of mistaken identity

What's going on here? Dr. Akins wondered. She glanced at her white smock and name tag and realized what had happened. Mrs. Arbuckle had previously mistaken her for a staff member.

You see, Mrs. Arbuckle had two personalities: a Dr. Jekyll and a Mrs. Hyde. The impatient, ill-mannered Mrs. Hyde that the staff knew became an ingratiating Dr. Jekyll in the veterinarian's presence. *No wonder my employees hate to see certain clients,* Dr. Akins thought.

Luckily, not all clients are like Mrs. Arbuckle. But just a

few like her can drive even a well-trained, dedicated staff crazy. Staff members often get caught between the proverbial rock and a hard place. They try to meet their employer's expectations, often while trying to cope with difficult clients who view them not as paraprofessionals but as annoyances.

We expect our employees to get along with our clients, to get their jobs done quickly and efficiently while maintaining a professional yet friendly manner. Meanwhile, they must deal with the duplicity of Jekyll-and-Hyde clients. These clients demand VIP treatment—preferably only by the veterinarian—and seem to regard everyone else as underlings.

But it doesn't have to be this way. Let's consider a few things you can do to build up your staff members so clients will treat them with the respect they deserve.

Clients follow your lead

Your attitude toward your staff influences how others see and treat them. Think about how you regard your employees. Are they merely extra pairs of hands, just the "girls" or "guys"—a necessary part of the practice but not much more important than the equipment or the building?

Or do you think of your staff as an integral part of your team—trained paraprofessionals, valued employees who not only help the business but are enjoyable to work with? How you regard and relate to your staff will directly affect your clients' actions toward them.

A more subtle yet equally important question to consider: How do your employees think you feel about them? Do you believe your staff is the greatest group of employees ever? Do you tell them you appreciate them? Or do you criticize, always pushing them to try harder? If so, they may feel they'll never win with you. If you believe your employees are inferior, don't be surprised if many of your clients treat them that way, too.

One of the most obvious ways you show your perceptions to others is in the way you talk to and about your staff. Have you uttered such phrases as "I'll have one of my girls take Siegfried back" or "My kennel boy will cut your dog's nails"? Although such remarks might not seem important, they convey the message that you view your employees as inferior.

Powerful first impressions

Your clients perceive you as a professional, an authority, and an expert. But they don't necessarily see your staff through the same lens. It's your job to ensure that they do. One of your best opportunities is when you introduce a staff member to a client. Remember, first impressions last.

Your staff members can make a powerful first impression in several ways. Do they dress like professionals? Do you provide them with clean, snappy uniforms or smocks? Are your employees clearly identifiable with your hospital, or might they be confused with other clients or people who just walked in off the street?

To alleviate this problem, use name tags that display your hospital's logo as well as the employee's title. This inexpensive gesture will help clients recognize the staff as part of the medical team.

A bulletin board is another simple, cost-effective way to share information about your staff with your clients. Display photographs of all staff members, identify their roles in the hospital, and supply a short paragraph about their interests and credentials. For example, if you employ a registered technician who trained in a two-year program, don't hide this fact—advertise it. If your technician wasn't formally trained but has worked for veterinarians for 10 years, tell your clients. Is your college diploma hanging on a wall somewhere in the hospital? How about displaying your technicians' certificates as well?

Another effective way to promote your employees is to warmly and respectfully introduce them to your clients. You could say: "You've already met Donna, our head receptionist, who showed you into the exam room. She's been with us for more than eight years. You can always count on Donna to greet you with a smile, because she loves people just as much as she loves their pets."

Or you might say: "I'd like you to meet Fred, one of our trained technicians. He'll take excellent care of Misty during her stay in the hospital. Fred's been a veterinary technician for more than five years, not counting two years of specialized study at Sanford Technical Institute, where he received his diploma as a certified veterinary technician."

Sound funny? It might at first, especially if you've thought of Fred only as "the young kid who helps out" and Donna as just "one of the girls." But by introducing staff members in a respectful manner, you'll raise their self-esteem and your appreciation for them as well. You'll also find your clients' perception of value will soar.

Don't ignore soft-tech training

Most veterinarians realize the importance of providing their employees with ongoing technical training. But they often miss the equally need for "soft-tech" training in such people skills as communication, professional presentation, self-esteem, and professional selling.

Carl Stevens, a nationally recognized motivational speaker, emphasizes the importance of strengthening professional communication skills, which he likens to a pair of scissors. Many professionals spend years sharpening their technical skills while ignoring their people skills. He says that's like trying to cut a sheet of paper with only one half of the scissors—it's not very effective.

The same holds true for your staff members. Investing a little time and money in developing their ability to communicate and relate to people will pay off. The next time a Jekyll-and-Hyde client walks through your door, your staff will have the confidence to handle the situation—and demonstrate the vital role they play in your hospital.

EXERCISE

Imagine you're a client and observe your staff from that perspective.

1. Walk through your hospital's front door one morning and ask yourself these questions:
   • Are staff members dressed professionally?
   • Do they wear name tags that are easy to read?
   • Do your employees act as professionally as you'd expect them to if you brought your pet to the hospital?
   • Do you have displays that help clients get acquainted with your team members?

2. Spend a day listening to how your employees refer to themselves and become conscious of how you refer to them. Practice introducing your staff as valued members of a professional team.

Section

<<<<<<<<<>>>>>>>>>

THREE

<<<<<<<<<>>>>>>>>>

The Big Picture

CHAPTER 15

<<<<<<<<>>>>>>>>

It's Time to Practice
ON PURPOSE

By defining what you want from practice, you will lead your team with renewed direction—and have more fun.

> "This is the true joy in life—the being used for a purpose recognized by yourself as a mighty one; the being a force of nature instead of a feverish, selfish clod of ailments and grievances, complaining that the world will not devote itself to making you happy."
> —George Bernard Shaw

Those words seemed harsh when I read them in 1988, but old George wasn't known for mincing words. The quote troubled me—until I realized why I found it so disturbing. The "feverish, selfish clod of ailments and grievances" part fit me to a "T."

After spending nearly 13 years in practice, most of them in my own small animal hospital, I'd turned into just the clod Shaw describes. Oh, I did most of my complaining quietly, either to myself or to my wife. Most of the people around me would've said I'd done pretty well in the Great American Dream Game. I had a lovely wife, nice home, two big cars, and had recently moved my practice into a new building that I'd designed. I was winning.

Except I'd find myself awake late at night. My thoughts echoed like Peggy Lee's old song, "Is That All There Is?"

Shaw's quote started me thinking: *What's my purpose? Why am I on the planet? Is it just to make money and have more expensive toys? What do I want to leave behind after I'm gone?* Such questions didn't help my insomnia, but they began to help me shape my life.

We all have a purpose in life—a reason for being here. Of course, your purpose may not be the one you're living now. We often start out with "inherited" purposes—goals that are determined by the society into which we were born.

It's not that I didn't have a purpose before reading Shaw's quote. At the time, my life was being shaped by what I believed was my reason for living—to make a lot of money, be comfortable, and retire early. But it wasn't enough. I kept asking, "Is this all there is?"

Shaping your life

Developing a life purpose involves more than making New Year's resolutions that are quickly forgotten—you use it as framework to build your life. Before I continue, I want to clarify two terms people often confuse: purpose and mission. Your life purpose is who you are, not what you do —it's who you are at work, at home, and in your community. Your life mission, on the other hand, is how you intend to fulfill your life purpose.

While working with Judy Billman, the business coach who had introduced me to Shaw's quote, I defined my life purpose to be "Making a difference with people." Although I've continually refined my life purpose since 1988, that first draft immediately began to shape my life.

My mission—or what I was doing to fulfill my new purpose—continued to be "Practicing the highest quality of veterinary medicine possible." At the same time, my writing became more important to me because I realized it also would enable me to fulfill my purpose.

Why have a life purpose? Because defining who you are and what your purpose is—then living it—empowers you through what I call the "four F's": focus, fulfillment, fun, and flow. Here's what I mean:

Focus. Developing a life purpose clarifies your priorities. After determining that my purpose was to make a difference with people, whenever I faced a new situation, I asked myself: *Is this consistent with my purpose?* If the answer was yes, I continued. If it was no, I stopped what I was doing and took an appropriate action for the situation—one that was consistent with my new purpose. I began to experience a renewed focus in my life.

Fulfillment. I also became much more fulfilled with the direction of my life. Now my life was about something I'd chosen, not something I'd inherited. People began to notice the changes, and I started hearing them acknowledge the difference I was making. Each time I heard a compliment, I'd think, *Wow! I'm doing it. I'm fulfilling my life purpose.*

Fun. My practice became a lot more fun as well. Now I was doing what I loved to do and fulfilling my life purpose. In many ways, my day-to-day activities hadn't changed appreciably. I still was spaying cats and dogs, expressing anal sacs, and clipping nails. But now I wasn't doing it just to make more money or my inherited purpose. I was making a difference with people and their pets—my chosen purpose.

Flow. As a result of all these changes, my practice and my personal life began to flow smoothly. During the next year, I made a huge difference with a lot of people—so many, in fact, that my practice grew more than 40 percent. In addition, my income more than doubled, even though I was working fewer hours with the same-size staff. While fulfilling my new life purpose of making a difference, I inadvertently was accomplishing my old purpose of making money. Life is funny that way.

Determining your purpose

So how do you determine your life purpose? Start by asking: "What's my life for—what's my purpose?" But forget the notion that there's only one "right" purpose. If you don't, you'll get stuck for sure.

While developing my own purpose and in working with many others, I've found it's a process that unfolds over time, like a blooming rose. The important thing is to take those first steps; then keep on stepping. A good way to develop a clearly stated purpose for your life is to ask yourself the kind of questions I'd asked myself:

- Why am I on the planet?

- At the end of my life, what do I want to be known for? (Although it may seem morbid, write your own eulogy. What would you like others to say about you at your funeral? Try it—it's a most interesting exercise.)

- If I could be remembered 500 years after my death, what would it be for?

- What am I known for now?

- How does what I'm known for compare with what I'd *like* to be known for? (You may discover you're already living your purpose, and just hadn't noticed it.)

Another way to clarify your purpose is to take a "back-door" approach. What I mean is that even though your life purpose is who you are and not what you do, you often can get in touch with your purpose by thinking about what you enjoy doing most.

Ask yourself the following questions, and write down your responses; then discuss the questions with others:

• What do I most enjoy doing with my time?

• If I had unlimited money, time, talent, and energy, what would I be doing with my life? (If you're overworked like many business owners, your first response may be: "Take a long vacation." That's fine, but after spending time traveling, loafing, and reading that stack of books on your night table, what would you do with your life?)

• What do I love to do so much that I'd be willing to do it for free? You may already be doing this activity as a volunteer or as a hobby. It's something you do for the joy of it, not to make a living.

• What are my unique talents and skills, and what am I really good at that I also love doing? Be sure to consider both aspects of this question. You may be really good at doing your taxes, for example, but you may not be particularly fond of the task.

Now, review your answers. Look for the common thread that runs through the activities you enjoy most. This exercise helped me refine my life purpose so that it presented a clearer and more focused expression of who I am. I changed "Making a difference with people" to "Assisting people in determining their life purpose and living their lives consistent with that purpose."

As I continued to explore the subject of purpose, I realized that the most powerful and long lasting purposes are those that are more about who we are than just what we do. This led to my purpose being redefined to living an inspired, inspired and courageous life of service, a life of mindful abundance balanced with simplicity, and a life of spiritual serenity. Now, all that I do as a writer, life and business coach, and speaker can be expressions of my life purpose. In fact, my life purpose has to the power to shape and form all my life.

These insights eventually led me to co-founding Life On Purpose Institute with my wife, Ann. (See the resource area at the end of this book for more information.)

Put your purpose on paper

The next step is to develop a clear statement of your life purpose. Why do you need such a statement? Because your life purpose will be much more powerful when you can state it clearly.

As you work on fulfilling your life purpose, you'll have to involve many other people. To help you, they will need to know who you are and what your life is about. When you have your purpose stated in one or two sentences, you can adapt it easily to the people with whom you're talking.

If I were talking to a group of high-school students, for instance, I'd probably state my life purpose this way: "I love helping young people figure out what they want to do with their lives." By phrasing my purpose this way, students would be more likely to seek me out after the talk, giving me another opportunity to fulfill my purpose.

It's also easier to keep the purpose alive if it's clearly written. Otherwise, you'd soon find yourself slipping back into your old, inherited purpose—just like forgetting New Year's resolutions.

Take it to heart

The best way to nourish your purpose is to begin developing commitments in each area of your life. Many of these will be existing projects you reformulate to fit your new purpose. You'll also want to think of other ways to express the "new you." The next chapter will guide you in that part of your journey.

As you line up your life with your purpose, don't be surprised if you experience a new level of focus, fulfillment, and fun. And don't be amazed when your life starts to flow with ease and grace. Living on purpose is like that.

EXERCISE

Develop a rough draft of your life purpose statement and try it out for the next two to three weeks. If you find that the statement doesn't empower you, write a new one. The next chapter will be much easier to understand if you do this exercise first.

CHAPTER 16

<<<<<<<<<>>>>>>>>>

Balancing Your Business and Your Life

If you're like most business owners, you're pulled in many directions. A life purpose statement can bring much-needed clarity.

"I am of the opinion that my life belongs to the whole community, and as long as I live, it is my privilege to do for it whatever I can.

I want to be thoroughly used up when I die for the harder I work the more I live. I rejoice in life for its own sake. Life is no "brief candle" to me.

It is a sort of splendid torch which I've got to hold up for the moment and I want to make it burn as brightly as possible before handing it on to future generations."

—George Bernard Shaw

Shaw's quote points to the power of bringing a life purpose to each area of your life. I found that while in practice, it was easy for me to forget that I belonged to the "whole community." I was suffering from a bad case of tunnel vision: The community in which I was involved often seemed to extend only as far as the four walls of my hospital.

When I learned about the concept of a life purpose, I also learned about the Wheel of Life—an easy and effective way to evaluate how balanced my life was or wasn't. While I didn't particularly like what the wheel revealed, it did give me a new perspective from which to look at myself, as well as a tool to balance my "whole community." We'll now examine how the power of a life purpose affects how you live—in and outside of your business.

What does the wheel reveal about you?

In the Wheel of Life, each spoke represents important areas of your life such as family, career, health, and community. I've labeled these areas in the example below, but you can add or substitute or create your own categories. Consider the part of the spoke closest to the hub as "0" and the part closest to the rim as "10," with 10 being ideal. Now rate yourself on the amount of time you spend on each area, the satisfaction you gain from it, and how well this area is working for you. Placing a dot along each spoke to represent the number you have determined. When you've finished, connect the points to see your wheel of life.

Ideally, the wheel you draw will be round and balanced. If it is, congratulations. My wheel, however, was so out of balance it looked as if I was about to have a blowout. I rated low in almost every area except career, even though the other areas were also important to me as well.

At the time, I spent 50 to 60 hours a week at my clinic—not counting the time I spent at home worrying about it. In the eight years I'd owned my practice, my involvement in my church had ceased, I'd stopped working out, I rarely did anything that could be called recreational, and most of my time at home was spent either arguing with my family or talking about the problems at work. It was clearly time to have my wheel of life realigned.

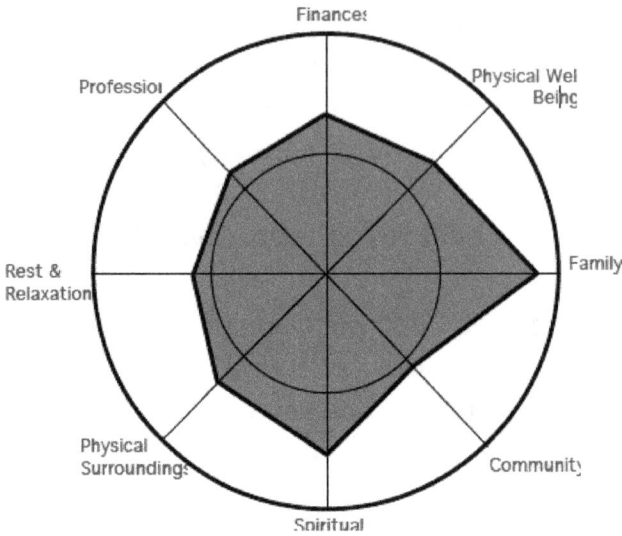

Finances / Physical Well Being / Family / Community / Spiritual / Physical Surroundings / Rest & Relaxation / Professional

Align your life with your purpose

If your life feels out of alignment, you can apply the principle of purpose to bring it back into balance. I realize this process isn't as easy as aligning the wheels of your car, but with a little attention and patience, I think you'll be surprised how quickly you can find balance.

If you find this exercise uncomfortable, keep in mind that life changes often are unsettling. If you're unbearably uncomfortable, however, simply ease off the throttle. After you've gotten used to a few of the changes, you can resume a safe speed. Here's how to begin:

1. Evaluate the areas where you're already expressing your life purpose. If you haven't done so, take some time now to decide what you'd like your purpose to be. Understand that by life purpose we mean who you are not just what you do. People often confuse a life purpose with a career or profession. I am not referring to this here. I am talking about a life purpose that includes all of your life. So give it a go. Nothing is set in stone—you're merely creating a rough draft that can be modified or discarded later. (If you are still uncertain about what your life purpose is and you would like to clarify it more distinctly, then visit www.lifeonpurpose.com for ways to clarify your life purpose.)

Now look at each category on the Wheel of Life and write down the various ways you currently express your purpose. You may have more than one response for some areas and none in others. That's OK. At this point, you're only evaluating.

This exercise may uncover projects you're doing that are no longer consistent with who you are. You can either stop them or adapt them to your purpose. For example, when I shifted my life purpose from "making money and being comfortable" to "making a difference with people," I didn't suddenly shut down my clinic. Instead, I designed my work in my practice to fall within my new purpose. Later, I sold my practice when I saw the possibility for greater fulfillment by devoting my efforts to writing, public speaking and life purpose coaching.

2. Look for new ways to express your purpose in each area of your life. You don't have to commit to any of these ideas, just explore the possibilities. If you find yourself getting excited about these areas, in a way you haven't been for some time, you're on-track. When you finish this step, you'll have a list of possible projects for each area of your life.

After you've written down your thoughts, ask yourself: Which projects seem the most exciting? Which seem to express the purest form of my purpose? Which would give me the most enjoyment?

3. Choose the projects to pursue. At this stage, you may be so excited about these new projects that you want to take them all on at once, or you could be so overwhelmed that all you want to do is take a nap. Most likely you fall between these two extremes.

Keep in mind that taking on new projects in every area at once will overwhelm you, no matter how enthusiastic you are about accomplishing them. On the other hand, if you decide every new project is too much trouble, you'll give up and get nowhere. I recommend taking on no more than three projects at a time. If you want to stretch a lot, pick three; if you want to stretch a little, pick only one. Keep the list handy and refer to it often.

You'll benefit the most by choosing projects in those areas most out of balance. For example, if you scored yourself 8 in career but only 3 in family, choose a project that allows you to spend more time with your family. If you're a born-workaholic like me, that may be tough to do. But remember, pursuing your life purpose without seeing the big picture can be just another way to keep your life out of balance.

Reap the rewards

The more effective you become at living your life purpose, the more you will attract others with similar interests. While these people may not have an identical purpose, they'll see that working with you helps them fulfill their own purpose. Everyone will gain from the experience.

EXERCISE

Draw your own Wheel of Life, then evaluate it:

1. If your wheel is out of balance, refer to your life purpose statement and identify one to three projects that will help you get it aligned. Be sure to choose projects with specific, measurable results, and decide a timeline to complete the projects.

2. Think of someone in your life who can help you fulfill these projects. Finding a partner is a great way to stay committed to your goals.

CHAPTER 17

<<<<<<<<>>>>>>>>

Slow Down!
You're Moving too Fast

Want to jump off the endless treadmill and spend more time on other interests? You can—if you learn to become debt-free.

His white-knuckled fingers gripped the side of the counter. I'd seen Dr. Brock stand there countless times before, but never like this. His face and neck were an angry red; his neck muscles strained. Beads of sweat welled on his brow, which was dry only moments before.

Allison, the technician, whispered, "Go get Mrs. Brock." Someone hurried away, relieved to escape the scene. Frozen to the spot, I didn't know what was happening or what to do. I was just an intern preparing for my senior year in veterinary school by spending a few weeks at the clinic learning what a "real practice" was like.

In a few minutes, Mrs. Brock appeared. She sized up the situation with a glance and nodded for the staff to leave Dr. Brock and her alone. Gratefully, we obliged. Allison took a deep breath as we headed toward the reception area. I suddenly realized I hadn't been breathing either.

"He'll be all right," Allison said. "He gets that way sometimes. The demands of the practice get to be too much for him. Mrs. Brock always manages to calm him down.

Thank goodness. I don't know what he'd do without her."

That scene, which took place the summer of 1973, is etched in my mind. I also remember the vow I made: *I'll never let my practice get the best of me. I'll quit first.* And yet at the helm of my own practice years later, days came when I was the doctor gripping the side of the counter, fighting for control. Caught in the frenetic pace, I felt like a hamster in a wheel, running as fast as I could to nowhere.

Fighting for control

Burnout is one of the most serious and common threats business owners face today. The condition takes many forms and produces various side effects. To escape its grip, you must pause from time to time and think about where you're going and what kind of life you're building. Perhaps even more important, why are you building it?

There's a quiet movement afoot in America that addresses these questions. Some call it downsizing, right-sizing, or simplifying your lifestyle. I like the term "DOMO." According to Sid Lerner in *Trash Cash, Fizzbos and Flatliners: A Dictionary of Today's Words* (Houghton Mifflin, 1993), DOMOs are "downwardly mobile professionals who abandon a successful or promising career to concentrate on more meaningful or spiritual activities."

Now, don't get me wrong. I'm not suggesting you abandon your successful and promising career to meditate on a mountaintop. Rather I'm saying it's time for Americans to examine what's driving us—a country that represents 5 percent of the world's population but consumes more than 30 percent of its resources.

To bring this statement closer to home, ask yourself: "What am I building, and why am I building it?" As many of today's DOMOs are discovering, it's possible to live an incredibly fulfilling life without working 60 to 70 hours a week—and without feeling deprived.

Joseph Dominguez, co-author with Vicki Robin of *Your Money or Your Life* (Viking, 1992), said the American dream wasn't always just about materialism, but somewhere we wandered off course, equating a large home, fancy cars, and exotic vacations with happiness. During the 1970s to the '10s, many of us learned the hard way that money doesn't buy happiness. Some of us are still learning this lesson.

What's driving you?

One way to get off the spinning wheel for a while is to ask yourself the questions below. Spend time on these questions. Don't look for the "right" answers because these are not those kind of questions. Rather, these questions are designed to help you uncover the unconscious motivations that drive you in your life. If you honestly explore these questions, you may discover it's time to change the direction of your business and other areas of your life as well.

1. Are you running your business, or is it running you?

2. When was the last time you took at least a one-week vacation? While on that vacation, did you spend much of the time worrying about the business?

3. What directs your business: your values or your lifestyle?

4. Do family members regularly ask for more of your attention?

5. Is your time at work satisfying and fulfilling, or do you often feel harried or bored?

6. Are you satisfied with the number of hours you work, or do you wish you could cut back?

7. When was the last time you sat down with your family and examined the direction of your life? When was the last time you examined the direction of your practice with your employees?

If your answers reveal you're not satisfied with the direction of your business and the motivation driving it, consider correcting your course.

Something doesn't feel right . . .

At the height of my business I lived in a beautiful four-bedroom home on almost two acres of land. My spacious deck overlooked a small stream, and two late-model, top-of-the-line automobiles sat in the driveway. I was living the great American dream—or so I thought. But most of the time I was so busy at my practice I didn't notice how unhappy I was. My wife and I both worked full-time jobs. I worked a regular shift and she worked the second shift, so we saw each other only on weekends.

One Sunday I walked out on my deck and gazed at the shimmering brook below. Suddenly I realized I'd been working so hard it had been months since I'd enjoyed my deck, my house, or my cars. There was definitely something wrong with this picture.

Such a consumer-driven life is common in today's consumer-driven culture. "Yearning for Balance," a survey conducted by the Merck Family Fund, reported that "a large majority of Americans say they have more possessions and are more financially secure than their parents were—yet less than half say they're happier." What would make these people more satisfied? Most respondents wanted to "spend more time with my family and friends." Very few put a high priority on having "more nice things in my home," "a bigger house," or "a nicer car." In fact, some people have so much stuff that hoarding has become a problem.

A highly consumer-driven lifestyle can put heavy demands on a business. For example, say you generate 25 percent net income in your practice. That means for every dollar you take home you must earn $4—and that doesn't account for the weighty tax burden most business owners carry. To make matters worse, most people actually "rent" their lifestyles—and at alarmingly high rates.

Too little time, too much debt

What I'm about to suggest may fly in the face of everything you've ever learned about the power of using OPM—Other People's Money. America is a land of debtors.

"Debt is part of the fabric of American life," says Joseph Mocera, author of *A Piece of the Action: How the Middle Class Joined the Money Class* (Simon & Schuster, 1994). "We see it, we want it, we buy it, even if we don't have the money for it."

Unfortunately, most of us pay an incredibly high interest rate for a lifestyle that doesn't provide the satisfaction and peace of mind we seek. Instead, the lifestyle locks us into working 50, 60, or more hours per week—not much of a return.

Before we discuss how much you pay to "rent" your current lifestyle, examine your business and personal finances, then determine how much you pay on outstanding personal debts. Include everything—your charge cards, car payments, student loans, home mortgages, and any other installment loans. Then do the same with your business finances, calculating your total monthly payments for all business debts. Now add together your personal and practice debts. Does the total shock you?

For many of us, debt is a major force that keeps us running on the vicious cycle of life. Madison Avenue, with the whole-hearted support of the television industry, does everything it can to convince us to keep being good consumers. But it *is* possible to jump off without suffering poverty or deprivation. In fact, people who've simplified their lives and become debt-free say they feel more fulfilled, satisfied, and prosperous than ever before.

In my experience, the vicious cycle starts to slow down when you begin to let your individual value system—rather than a high-consumer lifestyle—govern how you run your business and your life. The starting point is to get clear about your values.

Take a moment to think about what's really important to you — your values, those qualities that make your life worth living. Make a list of the top 10. For example, is honesty important to you? How about integrity, punctuality, family, community? At this point, don't be too concerned about whether your life reflects these values, just list them. Another way to discover your values is to ask yourself, "What do I stand for?" Or, "What values would I like to instill in my children?"

With your list in hand, you can now appraise your professional life honestly. Remember, don't be judgmental. Just try to determine how much your values and your lifestyle drive your business and how much your values do. It's not unusual to find a mixture of both. Whatever your appraisal turns up is OK. It gives you a starting place.

Put your values first

Letting your values drive your business can be powerful and exciting, but like any process it takes time. To begin, select a value that is particularly important to you yet lacking in your business. Say you choose integrity. Think about what integrity means to you. I see it as keeping your word, being true to your standards and ideals, and being true to yourself.

Next, make a list of the areas where integrity, or whatever value you've chosen, is present and where it's missing. List the steps you could take to bring more of it to your practice. Do this exercise for each of the values you listed.

Now, pick four or five areas in which you feel a particular value would be most effective, and establish a time frame for action. Write down a realistic completion date for each, then repeat this step for all 10 values.

This process is an exercise in integrity. In the end, your life will be consistent with who you are. By injecting your values into your business and life you'll take away much of your lifestyle-driven motivation. Now let's take a look at how you can speed up the process.

Once you have a clear sense of what's truly important to you you're ready for the next step: becoming debt free so that you will be in a position to focus on your values, not worry about your bills.

Financial freedom can be yours

The first time I was asked to add up my debt, I was afraid of the answer. But when I finally did the exercise, I was relieved to find that, although it wasn't a small amount, it didn't come close to the national debt.

After you figure your total debt, your challenge is to think of that number merely as the amount of money you owe other people. It's neither good nor bad. Financial experts say you can't handle your finances unless you know the facts. And most people simply don't know the facts.

The next move is to do something about it. Here's a simple method of eliminating debt that's worked for many people. I call it the "snowball" approach. It begins with your list of personal and practice debts. If your practice is a sole proprietorship, you may find it useful to lump all your debts together. If you're in a partnership or corporation, however, it's best to segregate your practice and personal debts. Unless your partners agree to work with you on this plan, tackle your personal debt first.

Make a list of your debts, putting the lowest amount at the top and the highest amount at the bottom. If you're like most people, your credit cards will be at the top and your home mortgage at the bottom. To start the snowball rolling, pay off as much as you can on your smallest debt while paying the minimum on the others. When you wipe out that first debt, continue to the next smallest debt. To work even faster:

• **Redirect the money you're saving.** If you pay 15, 18 percent or more in interest on credit-card balances while socking away money that's only earning 1 to 2 percent, you're actually losing money. Focus on one thing at a time. By paying off your debt, you'll have extra money to save.

• **Don't accumulate more debt.** This step is vital. Unless you're willing to stop living on credit, you'll sabotage the entire plan. For most people, this step means cutting up their credit cards. If you must keep one for emergencies, store the paid-up card where you can't get to it easily—in a safe-deposit box or frozen in a block of ice. Vow to use it only for a crisis.

• **Examine your spending habits.** Look for unconscious spending—money you spend that doesn't enrich life. Once committed to becoming debt-free, most people are surprised at how much money they can add to the snowball without feeling deprived.

Begin by looking at automatic debits to your checking accounts and credit cards. Businesses want to make it as convenient as possible for consumers to pay them because we make the minimum monthly payments unconsciously. It's like the gambling casinos turning your cold cash into plastic chips so you'll forget that every blue one is really $25.

After you pay off your first credit card, your snowball really picks up speed. Each time you pay off a debt, add the amount you were paying on that card to the minimum on your next debt. By the time you reach your mortgage, you'll have enough money to pay off two to three months' principal at a time. Remember, most of your mortgage payment in the early years is interest.

By using this method, most people are able to become debt-free within five to seven years. It's possible to do because our loan system limits debt to approximately 35 percent of annual income. If your debts exceed that amount, banks won't approve your home mortgage.

As your personal debt diminishes, the wheel slows down, and you'll find it easier to bring more of your values to your practice. Even better, you'll have more time for your family, more time to pursue your other interests, and more time to enjoy the real American dream—freedom from worry.

EXERCISE

Determine your total debt and decide which debt you'll pay off first.

1. Cut up your credit cards or put them someplace where you won't be tempted to use them.

2. Sit down with your family and brainstorm for ways to reduce expenses so that you can pay off your debt as soon as possible. If you are incorporating this into your business then meet with your staff and do the same thing.

3. Develop a simple scoreboard to track your progress.

Notes:

CHAPTER **18**

<<<<<<<<>>>>>>>>

Magic Moments!

"Moments of truth" can bond clients for life—or send them running out the door. Here's how to create a positive impression.

As Mrs. Marshall enters the foyer of the Slipshod Veterinary Clinic with her dog, Molly, on a leash, her nose wrinkles from the pungent odor. *Strike one,* she thinks, as she spies the mess another pet left earlier that morning. (Allen, the kennel assistant meant to get to it all morning.)

Mrs. Marshall approaches the counter in the waiting room, announcing that she's a new client. Kate, the busy receptionist, slides a new-client form across the counter to her, and without bothering to look up, says, "Please fill out all the lines, leaving nothing blank."

Fill it out with what? Mrs. Marshall wonders as she sits down. *Not only did that receptionist hardly acknowledge my presence, she didn't even offer me a pen. Two more strikes.* She opens her purse to look for a pen and almost dumps the contents on the floor when Molly tugs at her leash. Unable to see a place to hook the leash, Mrs. Marshall finally lifts one leg of her chair and places the loop of the leash under it.

Now, at least my hands are free, Mrs. Marshall thinks as she pulls a pen from her purse. Then she realizes she has another problem. *How am I supposed to fill out this form without something to write on?* she fumes to herself. Spying a cluttered pile of magazines on a nearby table (another project Allen keeps putting off), she picks one up and begins to fill out the form. Molly tugs at the chair.

A few moments later, Cindy, the technician, sticks her head out one of the waiting rooms. "Who's next?" Mrs. Marshall ignores her, thinking, *She couldn't be talking to me. I haven't finished filling out these forms.*

"Please come this way. We mustn't keep the doctor waiting," Cindy persists, finally drawing Mrs. Marshall's attention.

"But I haven't finished. . . ," Mrs. Marshall calls back, but the technician has already ducked back into the exam room, leaving the door open. Deeply frustrated, Mrs. Marshall walks over to the reception desk to return the form just as Rachel, the groomer comes around the corner, clutching a wet and angry cat by the scruff of the neck.

Spying one of her favorite play toys, Molly lunges for the cat, dragging the chair behind her. The chase is on as Rachel and the cat disappear around the corner with Molly and the chair in hot pursuit.

A shocked Mrs. Marshall stands frozen. She turns to the receptionist for help. "Please get my dog back," she pleads.

Kate glances at the form on the counter between them and replies, "I need for you to fill in all the lines before seeing the doctor."

"But, I didn't have time. . ." Mrs. Marshall begins, but before she can finish, the receptionist continues, "And in the future, you must restrain your pet while in the hospital."

A rocky start

OK, so maybe no veterinary clinic is as bad as that example.

Unfortunately, most of what happened to Mrs. Marshall isn't that uncommon. For every client visit there are dozens of "moments of truth"—situations that either produce a positive or negative experience. It doesn't matter whether the client is a faithful regular or a first-timer. If the negatives start to add up, the client will take his or her business elsewhere.

Experts say that the first two to three minutes are most critical in developing strong client relationships. I don't doubt that for a minute, and yet it would be a huge mistake to then ignore the next 10 minutes with the client—or the next 10 years. Many factors besides your technical expertise determine how satisfied clients are with your business.

To assess your moments of truth, consider these questions:

• **Is your facility pleasant to visit?** Few things make a negative first impression like a dirty or smelly animal hospital, so scrutinize your physical environment. I realize that not everyone works in a brand-new clinic, but that's no excuse for not making sure your hospital is clean, well-organized, and pleasant to visit.

I opened my first practice in a 30-year-old leased building painted Pepto-Bismol pink inside. Although it took my staff and I most of the first year to get the place presentable, the building's transformation attracted people in the neighborhood—who soon became our faithful clients.

• **Are you and your staff 'present and accounted for'?** Most of us have walked into businesses only to discover there was no one home. Receptionists may have been on duty, but when you talked to them, they weren't really with you. Even when they said all the right things— "Thanks for shopping with us…Have a nice day"—the words sounded impersonal.

It's easy to get caught up in the daily routine and become a "human doing" rather than a "human being." That was the receptionist's problem in the scenario at the beginning of this chapter. Although Kate was quite efficient at what she did, she didn't tune in to Mrs. Marshall—and that got the visit off to a rocky start.

• **Do you understand the client's perspective?** Sincerely empathizing with clients shows how much you care. Just imagine yourself in their shoes. How would you want to be treated? What concerns do you wish someone would consider? It might be as simple as a staff member offering to assist you. Or it might involve the receptionist asking you how your day was—and really listening to you.

Keep in mind that clients can be nervous about trying out a new service or business. It's doubly important to be sensitive to their feelings at such times.

• **Do you and your employees like your jobs?** People who work in service-oriented businesses often forget who they're supposed to serve. I once overheard a receptionist tell a co-worker, "I could sure get my job done a lot faster if all these people would just leave me alone." But people is what a business is all about. Without the people, there would be clients; without the clients, there would be no business.

• **How well do you communicate?** Effective communication can resolve just about any crisis. But that doesn't mean it's always easy. After all, most people avoid during difficult conversations, such as when someone makes a mistake.

For example, one of the worst moments in my veterinary career occurred when a client's dog escaped from my old clinic during a thunderstorm one night. We were treating the large German shepherd, named Bullet, for heartworms. I found out later that Bullet hated thunderstorms, so when the storm struck he freaked out and somehow managed to get out of his cage. Then he broke through a window.

When I arrived at the clinic the next morning, my staff was tense. They'd already scoured the neighborhood, hoping to find Bullet before I came in. Even a call to the animal shelter turned up nothing as well. There was only one thing left to do: call the owners.

A dozen different stories flew around in my head. Maybe I could claim that someone had broken into the clinic and stolen the dog, or maybe I could say Bullet had suffered a reaction to the heartworm treatment so we had to transfer him to the veterinary college. But even as I contemplated my options, I knew I had to tell the truth. After all honesty is one of my values.

So I made the call, praying for Mrs. Jerald to answer. I got along better with her than her husband.

No such luck. When Mr. Jerald answered, I took a deep breath, identified myself, and blurted out what had happened before I lost my nerve. On the other end of the line there was silence. When I thought I could stand it no longer, I heard the man laughing.

"I was wondering how long it would take you to call," he said. "Bullet was sitting on the front porch this morning when I went out for the paper. He sure hates being away from us during a thunderstorm. I'll bring him back as soon as I finish my breakfast." After that, the Jerald family became one of my most loyal clients.

The truth is, every moment may be a moment of truth. How your clients react to those moments in large part depends on you. My goal in writing this book has been to coach you in how to make the most of *every* moment of truth in you life — not only for your clients but for yourself, your staff, your clients, and your family and friends.

EXERCISE

Spend a week observing your practice as you look for and acknowledge both *magical moments* achieved by you and your staff and *not-so-magical moments*. Afterwards, debrief what you learn from your week of observation with your team during your next staff meeting.

Notes:

<<<<<<<<<<>>>>>>>>>>

Resources

Here are several additional resources for bringing more purpose and meaning to your life from Life on Purpose Institute, Inc.

Life On Purpose: Six Passages to an Inspired Life

Does the road to self-discovery really have to be so long and torturous? Not at all! Cut decades off the process and take a major shortcut on the road to clarifying your true purpose, says Dr. Brad Swift. Just follow the six steps, or "passages," that he outlines-and infuse purpose into every aspect of your life. Twenty years ago, Dr. Brad Swift appeared successful from the outside, but inside, he was burned out, wracked with emotional pain, and ready to end it all-because he was living at odds with his true purpose. But then he turned his life around to follow his true life calling, and in the process, invented this six-step method for determining one's life purpose.

He has since made a difference in the lives of hundreds of clients who've gone on to clarify their own purpose, and in many cases, teach this life-changing work. Have you clarified your life's purpose? Don't wait until your whole life has slipped by! This book can help you make a profound difference with your life.

Life On Purpose: Six Passages to an Inspired Life was an award winning finalist in the Self-Help: Motivational division of the Best Books 2007 Awards sponsored by USA

News. Order online at: **www.lifeonpurpose.com/lopbook.**

The Life On Purpose Virtual Video Coach

It's now possible to clarify your life purpose beyond a shadow of a doubt on your own time schedule, from the comfort of your home, or while driving to and from work, whenever it works best in your schedule. Since the Life On Purpose Process is divided into 6 discrete Passages, we have found most people can go through the whole program in from 6 to 12 weeks on average. But it's really up to you to decide what pace is best for you.

And since we all learn in different ways, the Virtual Video Coach combines visual learning, with auditory and kinesthetic learning modes. Complete information is online at: **www.lifeonpurpose.com/videocoach.**

Life on Purpose Certified Coaches

In the last decade the popularity of personal coaching has grown tremendously, as people discover the immense value of having a coach in their corner. Some of the benefits of having your own coach are:
- Focus—Your coach helps you stay focused on what's most important in your life.
- Clarity—Your coach can help you move from confusion to clarity.
- Confidence—When you see how much your coach believes in you, it helps build your confidence.
- Support Structure—Having regular coaching sessions gives you a structure for moving forward in your life.

Choose your coach at: **www.lifeonpurpose.com/coaches.**

Life on Purpose Coaches Mentoring Program

Creating a Global Community of the Most Effective and Successful Life Purpose Coaches in the World

Are you ready to make a profound difference in life? Do you long to make a profound and lasting difference with people? Does the idea of assisting people to clarify and live true to their life purpose call to you? Are you a coach searching for a proven, systematic approach to help people along their Purposeful Path? Do you yearn to be a part of a global community of like-minded people connected by a bold vision for transforming themselves and the world? Then you owe it to yourself to explore becoming a Life on Purpose Certified Coach. The Coaches Mentoring Program arose as a means for Life on Purpose Institute to fulfill its vision and mission:

The Vision: Life On Purpose Institute is a catalyst for creating a world on purpose.
The Mission: To deeply and profoundly touch and contribute to at least 1% of the world by assisting people to clarify and live true to their purpose.

Toward that end we are training some of the most effective and successful Life Purpose Coaches in the world. We have attracted a spiritually based community of people dedicated to transforming the world to a World on Purpose. Are you one of these people? How might you know?

A favorite quote of mine, from Frederick Buechner, will

help you answer that question: "Where your deep gladness meets with the deep hunger of the world, there you will find a further calling." Would it be your deep gladness to serve people as a Life Purpose Coach? Are you called to assist others in their transformation from the inside out, and at the same time to continue your own personal transformation? If so, you meet the basic requirement for becoming a Life on Purpose Certified Coach.

Find out more at: **www.lifeonpurpose.com/cmp.**

About the Author

For over two decades W. Bradford Swift has been conducting an experiment: "Is it possible to create a new context for life that is true to my deepest values, my sense of what's possible, and true to my soul and spirit? If it is possible, what will be the results? Will it enhance my life? Will I experience a true sense of purpose and meaning? Will I know at the end of the experiment that my life has mattered?"

Becoming a writer of visionary fiction and non-fiction has been an integral part of this experiment, as was co-founding Life On Purpose Institute with his wife in 1996, being a life coach to assist others to create their own life on purpose, and training other Life On Purpose Coaches.

Since selling his veterinary practice in the late 80's to pursue a career as a writer and life coach, Dr. Swift has published over 350 magazine articles in dozens of national publication. Many of these have been part of a pet writing project: *Project Purpose: to write and publish articles about people whose lives are dedicated to a bold and inspiring purpose or vision.*

He is also the author of visionary nonfiction including: *Life On Purpose: Six Passages to an Inspired Life, Spiral of Fulfillment: Living an Inspired Life of Service, Simplicity and Spiritual Serenity,* and *From Spark to Flame: Fanning Your Passion & Ideas into Money-making Magazine Articles that Make a Difference.*

Dr. Swift attended Clarion West in Seattle to further hone his skill and passion for writing fantasy and science fiction. These two genres are forms of visionary fiction – fiction that first and foremost entertains while also enlightening and encouraging the reader to embrace greater possibilities in their own lives.

Giving back to future generations of young adults and adults through visionary fiction and non-fiction is an integral part Dr. Swift's legacy of a life on purpose. To learn more about additional books by the author go to:

www.lifeonpurpose.com/books
and
www.lifeonpurpose.com/amazonpage

Porpoise Publishing
Flat Rock, NC 28731
www.lifeonpurpose.com
Library of Congress Cataloging-in-Publication Data

You're the Coach: The Transformational Power of
Business Coaching/ W. Bradford Swift.
ISBN-10:1-930328-02-8   ISBN-13: 978-1-930328-02-0
1. Business coaching 2. Practice management
3. Communication
Copyright © 2012, W. Bradford Swift

Author's photo by B. J. Condrey
Edited by Ann T. Swift
Cover Design by Ann T. Swift
Typeset in Palatino
Printed in USA

www.ingramcontent.com/pod-product-compliance
Lightning Source LLC
Chambersburg PA
CBHW060608200326
41521CB00007B/693